INDIA[■]

INDIANA

"Logansport, June 1837"
by George Winter

by
Alan McPherson

i

McPherson, Alan J. (James), 1947-
    Indian Names in Indiana/by Alan McPherson
112 p. also xvi (16) pgs. introduction, 15 cm., 3 mm. x 23 cm._____
Native American People _____Includes indexes, maps, illustrations
Summary: Lists geographical place names of Native American origin in
Indiana and their meaning.
1. Indian Place Names in Indiana — juvenile & adult literature. (1. Indian
Names in Indiana of New World origin.)
1. Indiana - Indians - Place Names.   2. Indians of North America - Place
Names -Indiana.   3. Place Names - Indiana - Indians.
    c. 1993 ISBN 0-9636978-0-3

Printer:
The Blasted Works
214 N. Main St.
Monticello, IN 47960
USA

Cover Illustration: "No-Wash-Moan (Rest), Pot-to-wat-ta-mie" color oil painting by George Winter, courtesy of the Tippecanoe County Historical Association. Gift of Mrs. Cable G. Ball. (M-71)

CONTENTS

ACKNOWLEDGMENTS

The author is indebted to the many individuals who have given freely, contributing to the compiling of this reference book of Indiana's Native American place names. Librarians and historical society staff members were especially helpful locating numerous resources.

I am also indebted to the following historical societies for their permission to feature historic illustrations from their collections which add distinction to the pages: Fulton County Historical Society, Howard County Historical Society, Indiana Historical Society, Northern Indiana Historical Society and the Tippecanoe County Historical Association.

The original pen and ink drawings are by Angie Neidlinger and Steve Hudson. All other photographs are by the author.

This book is dedicated to those first on the land!

THEIR CANOES HAVE VANISHED.

THEIR FORESTS FALLEN SILENT.

BUT THEIR NAME IS ON YOUR WATERS.

YE MAY NOT WASH IT OUT.

LYDIA HUNTLEY SIGOURNEY

**Mississinewa Battlefield Marker
& Poem Inscription Near Jalapa, Indiana**

"Ye say, they all have passed away,
   That noble race and brave;
That their light canoes have vanished
   From off the crested wave;
That, 'mid the forests where they roamed,
   There rings no hunter's shout;
But their name is on your waters,--
   Ye may not wash it out.

Ye say, their cone-like cabins,
   That clustered o'er the vale,
Have fled away, like withered leaves
   Before the Autumn gale;
But their memory liveth on your hills
   Their baptism on your shore,
Your everlasting rivers speak
   Their dialect of yore."

from poem ***Indian Names***
by Lydia Huntley Sigourney (1791-1865)

v

A LISTING: INDIAN NAMES IN INDIANA

Amboy
Anderson
Anoka
Aubbeenaubbee

Baugo Creek
Beanblossom
Ben Davis Fork
Black Hawk
Burnetts Creek, Burnettsville

Calumet
Cayuga
Cedar Creek
Charley Creek
Chili
Chippewanuck Creek
Churubusco
Clifty Creek
Coesse
Cornstalk
Cuba
Cuzco

Deer Creek
Delaware
Door Village
Driftwood

East Chicago, New Chicago
Eel River, north
Eel River, south
Elkhart
Erie

Fall Creek
Flat Rock
Flower's Creek

Georgetown
Greentown

Huron
Hurricane Creek

Indian
Indiana
Indianapolis
Iroquois

Jalapa

Kankakee
Kappa
Kewanna
Kickapoo Creek
Killbuck Creek
Klondike, Klondyke
Kokomo

LaCrosse
LaFontaine
Lagro
Lake Cicott
Lake Lenape
Lake Manitou
Logansport

Maconaquah
Majenica
Manhattan
Maumee
Maxinkuckee
Menominee
Metamora
Metea
Metocinah Creek
Mexico
Miami
Michigan
Minnehaha
Mishawaka

Mississinewa
Mixsawbah
Modoc
Mohawk
Mongo
Monon
Monoquet
Montezuma
Muncie
Muscatatuck River
Muskelonge Lake

Nappanee
Natchez
Nebraska

Ohio
Ontario
Opossum Creek, Opossum Run
Oregon
Osceola
Oswego
Otisco
Otsego
Owasco

Papakeechie Lake
Patoka
Parish Grove
Paw Paw Creek
Peoria
Peru
Pigeon River
Pipe Creek
Pokagon State Park
Potawatomi, Pottawattomi, Pottawattomie

Raccoon
Red Cloud
Roanoke, Roanoke Station
Russiaville

Salamonia, Salamonie
Saluda
Sandusky

Saratoga
Shakamak
Shankitunk Creek/Shankatank Creek
Shawnee
Shipshewana
Sitka
Squirrel Creek
Strawtown
Sugar Creek

Tecumseh
Thorntown
Tiosa
Tippecanoe
Topeka
Toto
Trail Creek

Vermillion

Wabash
Waco
Wadena
Wakarusa
Wanatah, South Wanatah
Wawasee, Waubee
Wawaka
Wawpecong
Wea
Weasel Creek/Weasaw Creek
Wells County
White Cloud
White Eye Trail
White River
Whitewater
Wildcat
Winamac
Winona, Winona Lake
Wolf Creek
Wyalusing Creek
Wyandotte

Yankeetown
Yellow River
Yorktown

ILLUSTRATIONS

ILLUSTRATIONS

ILLUSTRATIONS

ILLUSTRATIONS

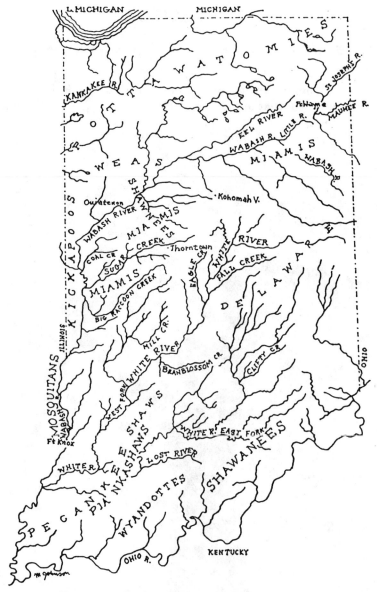

Map 1. 18th Century Indians in Indiana's Territory.
drawing by Mary Early Johnson.

PREFACE

This A to Z reference book lists over 100 Indian-derived place names in Indiana along with various historic interpretations regarding their origin and definition. Several are easily understood as to their meaning, but many are lost in history. Despite the studious endeavors of scholars, there remains a wide difference of opinion regarding Native American name sources and their significance. Much is open to conjecture. The focus herein is on compiled scholarly interpretation instead of complicated linguistical analysis. The author concedes a more in-depth research of the literature is warranted for greater accuracy and detail. A fertile imagination helps to enhance reading enjoyment and in many instances, the reader will draw his own conclusion.

There are several place names of American Indian origin in today's Indiana. Geographic names of villages, towns, cities, townships, counties, schools, parks, streets, streams and lakes have linguistic ties to the inhabitants who lived on the land at the time of European exploration of the Americas. The State and Capital namesakes commemorates the historic Indian tribes of Miami, Potawatomi, Shawnee, Delaware, Kickapoo and others who formerly occupied present-day Indiana less than two centuries ago.

The majority of Indian place names are indigenous to the tribes who resided here; however, several are from other regions of the United States and Canada as well as Central and South America. Streams were often given Indian names or translations thereof. Oftentimes the Euro-Americans applied Indian names to a place because they liked the unique sound, that their former home in the Northeast or South had the same name, or it reminded them of someone or something special.

For the most part, Indiana Indian tribes spoke different dialects of Central Algonquian; a linguistic family stock of Indian language spoken by most tribes of the northeastern United States and Canada. Algonquian-speaking historic tribes such as the Miami, Potawatomi, Delaware, Shawnee, Illinois, Menominee, Ottawa, and Chippewa, lived primarily along the major rivers and lakes. Additional Indian languages besides Algonquian that have left their mark on the state map include Iroquoian of the Northeast, Siouan from the West, Appalachian from the Southeast, Muskogean of the South, Caddoan from the Southwest, and Shoshonean from the Pacific Northwest.

Pure-sounding Indian names are a rarity. The Indians named persons, objects and places largely on account of some distinguishing characteristic, appearance or use. They did not have a written alphabet. The newly-arrived Euro-American explorers and pioneers sounded out and modified the Native American names to fit their own tongues. Usually they translated the Amer-Indian words to what they thought they meant in the languages of Spanish, French and English. These hybridized names are hardly recognizable from their original form and meaning. Slight change usually altered the Amer-Indian definition, which is now seemingly lost in antiquity.

There are places with Indian-sounding names, but these names are not truly Native American such as the French-derived Aboite or the Latin Amo. Peoga, Nyona and Numa also sound Indian, but they are names invented by European tongues. There are also place names that may have links to the original inhabitants such as Sassafras and Toto. Some are also places where the name has been "coined" or fabricated such as Indiana, Indianapolis and Indian Heights.

Northern Indiana is more punctuated with Indian place names than southern Indiana. Historians point out that early settlers north of the Ohio River, feared and hated the original occupants because of the threat of massacre. Thereafter, the settlers were reluctant to name their hard-won surroundings in the Indian's memory.

However, by the time northern Indiana was being settled, Indian resistance was minimal as they were forced further west. By 1830, the former occupants were viewed more as legendary romantic figures. Ear-catching and exotic-sounding Indian names became permanent fixtures on maps, particularly in the upper Wabash River Valley and its tributaries. Since there were no written Indian languages, names were phonetically sounded out and spelled as they sounded. Today, very few if any speak Algonquian in Indiana. The Native American population is Indiana is nearly 12,000, according to the 1990 U.S. Census.

The Indian names that dot our maps tell a history of the people who formally occupied the land we now call Indiana. The majority of Indian geographic names are descriptive. Many commemorate events, tribes and individuals. Some place names are for wildlife, and others for customs and ceremonies. The following list is by no means complete.

My personal interest in Indian names stems from childhood. Growing up in a small northern Indiana town with an Indian "place" name was a constant reminder of their former presence. Identifying most of these names and their meaning gives a historic sense of place and a better understanding of where and who we are.

Alan McPherson
Kewanna, Indiana

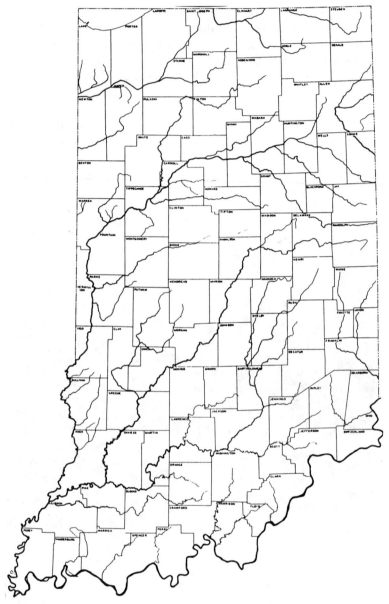

Map 2: Indiana Counties & Streams

AMBOY (AM-boy)
Town in southeast Miami County, est. 1867 (E-7)*

Amboy was platted after the Civil War as a shipping station of the Pennsylvania Railroad. The town site occupies high ground near the southeast bank of Honey Creek, a tributary of Big Pipe Creek which flows to the Wabash River. The place name commemorates the New Jersey community of Perth Amboy, Middlesex County; the former residence of the Scottish-born surveyor of the Indiana settlement, A.M. Goodrich.

Perth is a Scottish name for James, the Earl of Perth, Lord High Chancellor of Scotland, who held a royal land grant for the New Jersey settlement. The royal first half of the place name was dropped in egalitarian Indiana, leaving Amboy.

Amboy is belived to be a corruption of the Delaware Indian word, ompage, meaning "standing" or "upright" in reference to the level high ground the New Jersey community occupies at the mouth of the Raritan River, Raritan Bay and Arthur Kill Sound. Raritan Point was known as "ompage" to the Delaware, according to a 1651 deed.

Some writers derive the opposite meaning from Amboy. Instead of a level land shelf elevated above the surroundings, Amboy is derived from emboli and means "round or hollow like a bowl or basin."

ANDERSON (AN-dur-son)
City & township of central Madison County, est. 1823 (G-8)

William Anderson, son of a Delaware woman and Swedish-American trader, John Anderson, was born in a Delaware village along the Ohio River near Beaver Creek below Ft. Pitt, Pennsylvania, between 1750 and 1757. William Anderson's Delaware name was Kok-to-wha-nund, Kit-tha-we-nund, Kik-tuchwenind, Kiktowink, Keehlawhenund or Kiktutchwenind meaning "making a cracking noise," or "causing to crack" such as a tree about to fall in the forest. In later years he became a chief and he and his people came west to Indiana.

Several Delaware villages were situated along the Wapihanne or West Fork White River from Muncie to Noblesville, Indiana. Anderson's Town or Wah-pi-mins-rink or Wapiminskink, meaning "place of the chestnut tree," was located on the south side of the White River near present-day Anderson. John Anderson's trading post on the Delaware-named Susquehanna River near Marietta,

*(Letter - Number Locator corresponds to Indiana DOT State Highway Map.)

Pennsylvania, was also known as the "the chestnut place."

Chief Anderson or Koktowhanund was friendly to the American settlers. His daughter Oneahye or "dancing feather" married a pioneer settler. Anderson welcomed the Moravian missionaries who built a mission in 1801 at his village. In 1813, the village was burned by U.S. troops. The chief was the main voice of the Indiana Delawares at the Treaty of St. Marys, October 1818, whereby all remaining tribal lands were ceded to the United States. Anderson died in 1821 and his death remains a mystery.

The city of Anderson has a 1.5 mile Indian Trails Riverwalk near his former village site along the White River West Fork.

ANOKA (a-NO-ka)
Village in south central Cass County, est. 1876 (E-6)

More than likely, the place name Anoka is derived from the Dakota or Sioux people of the northern Mississippi River valley meaning "on both sides." The Ojibwa word anoki meaning "where they work," "the works," or "a busy place" is somewhat similar. The name was first applied at Anoka, Minnesota, where the town fathers laid out the county seat "on both sides" of the Rum River in 1853.

Twenty years later when the Cass County village was first platted, it was named Herman City, after the individual who did the platting, F. Herman Smith. The place name changed shortly thereafter to Anoka and is considered commendatory.

There are some local doubts whether the place name is either Indian or derived from Minnesota. However, modern day travellers driving through the Indiana community will find the name somewhat descriptive since Anoka is now situated "on both sides" of U.S. highway 35, three miles southeast of Logansport, Indiana.

AUBBEENAUBBEE (aw-bee-NAW-bee)
Township in northwest Fulton County, est. 1839 (C-6)

According to Dunn, Indiana historian, Au-be-naube translates to "looking backward" or "he looks back" as a person or animal looks backwards while moving or running. Aubbenaubbee may also mean "morning person" or "a mythic being." Spelling variants include Aubbeenaubbee, Aub-bee-naw-bee, Aub-bee-new-bee, Auu-be-nau-be, Awbenabi, Aubenabi, Aub-bee-naub-bee, Aub-bee-naub-ba, Obanaoby and Wabanaba.

Au-be-nau-bee was born around 1761 between the headwaters of the Kankakee and St. Joseph rivers in northern Indiana. He rose to chief of his band and in 1830 was granted a large reserve of thirty-six sections of rolling lake morraine country south of Lake Maxinkuckee, Marshall County.

Although most of his reservation was in Fulton County, Au-be-nau-bee frequented Kosciusko County and held lands in Clay, Harrison, and Prairie townships. Six years later, his lands were sold by the Treaty of Tippecanoe 1836.

Au-be-nau-be, Aubbeenaubee, Potawatomi Chief
drawing by C. Lee Jennings

His son, Pau-koo-shuck, avenging the death of his mother by Au-be-nau-bee, killed the chief in his cabin near the village of Richland Center, Indiana, in 1837 or 1838.

BAUGO CREEK (BAW-go-kreek)
Stream in southwest Elkhart County & southeast St. Joseph County (A-B-7)
Township in southwest Elkhart County, est. 1830 (B-7)
Park in east central St. Joseph County (A-7)

Dropping the first syllable, Baugo is an abbreviated version of the Potawatomi word, bau-bau-go or baw-baw-go, meaning "demon or devil river." The 20 miles of stream was considered swift and dangerous during heavy rains. An Indian foot trail followed the stream bank from the St. Joseph River, upstream to a village site at the junction of Apple Road and Dragoon Trail, south of Osceola, Indiana.

Baugo Creek flows northwest to join with the St. Joseph River due west of the Elkhart and St. Joseph county line at Ferrettie/Baugo Creek County Park, Osceola, Indiana. Visitors to the county park may walk segments of the former Indian foot path alongside the stream.

Bau-bau-go or Baugo Creek "demon or devil stream"

Little Baugo Creek forms in southwest Elkhart County flowing north and west of Wakarusa, Indiana, to join with Baugo Creek near the west central St. Joseph-Elkhart county line.

BEANBLOSSOM (been-BLAW-som)
Creek in north Brown & north Monroe counties (J-K-6-7)
Village in northwest Brown County, est. 1833 (K-6)
Lake in northeast Monroe County (K-6)
Township in northwest Monroe County, est. 1818 (K-6)

The name Beanblossom is a near translation of the Miami name, Ko-chio-ah-se-pe or "bean river." Hakiach-hanne is the Delaware name and Co-shes-po-we-set, the Huron name for the stream. The descriptive name provokes images of wild legumes that were sources of food, medicine, beauty and wonder to the Indians.

The headwaters lie west of Peoga, Indiana, (possibly Algonquian for "village") in northeast Brown County, south of Spearsville, Indiana. The stream waters flow west to form Lake Lemon or Beanblossom Lake, in northeast Monroe County and then on to Gosport, Indiana, where it joins with the White River West Fork, 51 miles later. The village, lake, and township are named for the stream.

The Miami name, Ko-chio-ah-se-pe or "bean river" is also the name of the St. Joseph River near Fort Wayne. Allen County, Indiana.

BEN DAVIS FORK (ben-DAY-vis-fork)
Stream of east central Rush County (H-9)

The Delaware knew this tributary of the Flat Rock River as mahoning, mahonink, mahonoi, mahanay or m'hoani "salt lick" or "where there is a lick" referring to their former Pennsylvania home river that had saline springs and deposits where deer congregated. The name was applied by the Delaware to many places having saline deposits. A main Delaware village existed in Union Township, Rush County, in the same area as the stream.

Ben Davis, the present name of the short stream was the English name of the Delaware warrior Chief Petchekekepon (b. 1780's?-d. 1820?), who resided in the area. He was a deadly foe of American settlers during the War of 1812 and was later killed by a revengeful survivor of one of his earlier war raids in Kentucky.

BLACK HAWK (BLACK-hawk)
Village in southeast Vigo County, est. 1903 (K-3)

Black Hawk is the condensed English name of Black Sparrow Hawk or Ma-ka-tai-me-she-kia-kiah (1767-1838), a Sauk leader and brave. He signed his name only once to a treaty in May 1816 at St. Louis, Missouri. His name has appeared as Ma-ka-tai-me-she-kia-kiah, Ma-ka-ta-mi-ci-kiak-kiak, Ma-ka-tai-me-she-kia-kiak, Mamakatawimesheka-kaa, Ma-ka-mi-ci-kiak-kiak, Meek-a-tah-mish-o-kah-kiak, and Mucketa-machekaka. His English name is derived from his wearing black sparrow hawk feathers (American Kestrel, Falco Sparverius).

Makataimeshekiakiah or Black Hawk, Sauk Leader
painting from
Thomas L. McKenney & James Hall

In ths spring of 1832, Ma-ka-tai-me-she-kai-kiah and 900 of his people returned to their native Illinois from Iowa. The Sauks wanted to live in peace but having once joined Tecumseh to push back American advancement in Ohio and Indiana, they were seen as a threat. Chased north into

Wisconsin, The Sauks were nearly annihilated by Federal troops near the mouth of Bad Axe Creek near Sauk City, August, 1832. After his capture, Black Sparrow Hawk became a celebrity. He returned to Iowaville, Iowa, where he died in 1838.

Black Hawk, Indiana, was named for commendable reasons. There was another village called Black Hawk in Shelby County, now called Mt. Auburn, Indiana, to avoid confusion with the Vigo County community. Erie Township, Miami County, was once called Black Hawk also in honor of the Sauk leader, but was changed to Erie to recognize the Wabash and Erie Canal that was built in the township.

BURNETTS CREEK (bur-NETS-kreek)
BURNETTSVILLE (bur-NETS-ville)
Stream of Cass, White & Tippecanoe counties (E-F-5-6)
Stream of White & Carroll counties (D-E-5-6)
Town in east central White County, est. 1836 (E-5)

Burnetts Creek is named for Abraham Burnett, who was of French-Potawatomi descent, the son of William Burnett and Cakima, Kawkeama, or Kaukema, daughter of Chief Anaquiba and sister to Chief Topenebee. According to the frontier artist, George Winter, Burnet was educated at the Choctaw Academy, Great Crossings, Kentucky.

Burnett was opposed to American advancement and supported Tecumseh. Despite his Indian support during the War of 1812, he received land in the Treaties of 1818 and 1826. Burnett's Reserve was located on two sections along the Wabash River in Adams Township, Carroll County. Burnett and his wife D'mouchekee-keeawh left for Kansas with his people in 1838. He died in Topeka, Kansas in 1871.

Burnett's Creek, that begins near the White-Carroll County line, flows southeast to the Wabash River near Lockport, Indiana. Burnettsville, Indiana, was named for the nearby stream. Additional land grants Burnett acquired include the site of the Battle of Tippecanoe and flowing nearby is a second Burnett's Creek, also named after him.

CALUMET (CAL-lu-mit)
Streams of LaPorte, Porter & Lake counties, Indiana, and Cook County, Illinois, (A-B-3-4-5)
Township in Lake County, Indiana, est. 1837 (A-3)

Nickname/sobriquet of the Indiana metropolitan Lake Michigan regional counties of Lake, Porter & LaPorte (A-B-3-4-5)

More than likely, Calumet is derived from the Norman-French word, chalemel, chalumet, or chalumeau meaning "little pipe," in particular a sheep herder's reed smoking pipe and the stem or shaft, possibly made from calamus (Aeorus calamus) reed. It may also be a French-Canadian corruption of the French word, calomo or "honey wood." The Franco-Americans applied the word to the ceremonial peace pipe of the North American Indians.

It is possible the name is derived from the Algonquian word calumic also spelled calumick, cal-la-mick, kil-la-mick and ken-no-mick and ken-no-mo-konk. The Potawatomi called the streams

"A Summer Evening in Vincennes"
painting by Augustus Lynch Mason

ken-nom-kyah and the Delaware knew the water bodies as gel-kel-e-muk. All of these refer to "a long body of deep still water." One source cites yet another Indian name for the Calumet streams, con-amic or "snow beaver."

The Little Calumet River heads in LaPorte County, flowing west through LaPorte, Porter, Lake counties, Indiana, and Cook County, Illinois, to its confluence with the Grand Calumet River. The Grand Calumet River heads at Long Lake in Lake County, Indiana, and flows west to northwest to Cook County, Illinois, and eventually Calumet Harbor at Lake Michigan.

CAYUGA (ka-YUU-ga)
Town in northeast Vermillion County, est. 1827 (G-3)

The Cayuga are one of the six nations of the Iroquois confederation, fomerly occupying the shores of Cayuga Lake, New

York, one of the Finger Lakes. A large number of the tribe moved to Canada during the American Revolution and the remainder were taken in by other tribes of the confederacy. (see Iroquois, Mohawk)

The Iroquoian-derived name is from gweu-gweh, gweh-u-gweh, gwa-u-geh, gwe-u-gweh, or gue-u-gweh-o-no and is believed to mean "the people of the mucky land." Additional translations include "long lake," "portage," "where they haul boats out," "the place where locusts were taken out," "taking canoe out at the Tonawanda portage" and "lake at the mucky land "

Cayuga, Indiana, was first known as Eugene Station. Evidently the name is a transfer from upstate New York. The nearby city and county in New York are named after Cayuga Lake.

CEDAR CREEK (SEE-dur-kreek)
Stream in western Dekalb & western Allen counties (B-C-9-10)
Township in central Allen County, est. 1825 (C-9-10)

Mes-kwah-se-pe is the Potawatomi word for Cedar Creek. The 40-mile-long stream originates in Dekalb County at Indian Lake, northwest of Corunna, Indiana, and flows southeast to join the St. Joseph River at Cedarville, Indiana, north of Ft. Wayne, Indiana. The Potwatomi Chief Mete-ah's or Metea's village was at the confluence of the stream and was known as Mes-kwah-wah-se-pe-o-tan or "Cedar Creek town." (see Metea)

According to Charles Deam, former state botanist,

Ancient Cedar at Mes-kwah-se-pe or Cedar Creek,

the eastern red cedar (Juniperus virginiana) in the virgin forest was restricted to high bluffs and banks of streams where it could compete with other plant species.

CHARLEY CREEK (CHAR-li-kreek)
Stream in central Wabash County (D-E-7-8)

The name commemorates Eel River Miami Chief Ken-ton-gah,

Ke-tun-ga, or "Sleepy" (b. ?-d. 1826?) who lived at the present-day city of Wabash, Indiana, in the village of Takingammeoongi, Takincomiong, Ta-king-ga-mi-un-qi, Tah-king-gom-me or Kin-com-a-ong meaning "cold running water place," also known today as Paradise Spring.

Ken-ton-gah preferred to remain neutral with both the Americans and British, but was loyal to the American cause. The chief signed the treaties of Vincennes (1803), Ft. Wayne (1809) and St. Marys (1818). The 1826 Treaty of Paradise Spring opened 650,-000 acres of northern Indiana and southern Michigan for settlement. Chief Ken-ton-gah or Charley and his family received six sections of land along the Eel River and in the town of Wabash near Paradise Spring.

Charley Creek begins near Lagro, Indiana, and flows southeast through the city of Wabash to the Wabash River.

CHILI (CHAI-lai)
Village in central Miami County, est. 1839 (D-7)

Chile is the older English spelling of Chili and was probably named after the South American nation since there were other exotic-sounding Latin American place names such as Mexico and Peru in Miami County.

The place name Chili is derived from the indigenous Quechua Indians and their word chilli or tehili meaning "cold or snow" or "the deepest point of the earth." The Quechua used it to designate the Aconcagua River and valley. Possibly the name may also be derived from the sound that the Chilean bird, trile (Turdus thilius) makes during flight, "chi-li, chi-li."

CHIPPEWANUCK CREEK (chi-pe-WAA-nuck-kreek)
Fifteen mile stream in southwest Kosciusko & north central Fulton counties (C-7)

The Potawatomi named this tributary of the Tippecanoe River, Chippewanuck, Chippewaynuck, Chipwahnuk, Chipwanic, Chippewanaung meaning, "Chippewa burial place" or "ghost spirit hole." Quite possibly the Potawatomi name refers to a mass grave of dead Chippewa and Potawatomi warriors. Che-pyuk means "spirit or ghost" and wah-nuk means "hole."

According to local legend, a hunting party of Chippewa (a name form of Ojibwa) warriors were massacred by the Potawatomi sometime around 1800, near the steam confluence.

It is also possible the Chippewa occupied the site since there are references to Chippewaynuck Village, a place where treaties were signed.

Chippewanuck Creek, "ghost spirit hole"
drawing by Angie Neidlinger

The small stream begins at the outlet of Rock Lake in Kosciusko County, flowing northwest. Mud Lake and other smaller lakes and farmlands contribute their excess waters to the stream which empties into the Tippecanoe River, southeast of Talma, Indiana.

CHURUBUSCO (che-ru-BUS-ko)
Town in northeast Whitley County, est. 1870 (C-9)

The selection of Churusbusco for the post office name did not come easily to the early residents of this northeastern Indiana town. The merger of two adjacent settlements, Franklin and Union in 1870, required a new community name. After much disagreement, the American battle victory site at Churubusco, Mexico, during the Mexican-American War in 1847, was selected.

The place name Churubusco is of Mayan-Aztec origin and means "hummingbird-on-the-left-side."

Es-the-nou-o-ne-ho-ne-que or, "decending from high rock"
Fall Fork of Clifty Creek, Anderson Falls

CLIFTY CREEK (KLIF-ti-kreek)
Stream in Rush, Decatur & Bartholomew counties (J-K-7-8-9)
Township in eastern Bartholomew County, est. 1821 (K-7)

Es-the-nou-o-ne-ho-ne-que or "cliffs or rocks river" or "decending from high rock" is the Miami name for Clifty Creek. Within a few miles the limestone stream bed descends several feet in elevation. The Delaware name, Esseni-ohanhokaqui, and the Huron name, Esthenounekenequa, have similar meanings.

The scenic stream originates in Rush County and heads southwest through Decatur and Bartholomew counties. The mouth of the stream is about 50 miles away from its source, emptying into the White River East Fork below Columbus, Indiana.

COESSE (ko-ES-see)
Town in southeast Whitley County, est. 1854 (C-9)

Coesse was the Potawatomi nickname of Me-tek-kah or M-tek-kyah, (17?-1853) or "burning the woods." The Miami Indian was

Me-tek-kah or Coesse, "burning the woods"

often called Coesse, pronounced Ku-wa-zi or Ko-wa-zi meaning "old man." The Miami also said Ku-wa-zi or Ko-wa-zi. His name is written on treaties as Coisa, Koessay, and Kowassee.

Me-tek-kah or Coesse was the grandson of Me-she-kin-no-quah or "Little Turtle" and the son of Me-kot-ta-mon-gwah or "Black Loon." Coesse was a nickname given to him as a young boy by his grandfather who had heard it from Potawatomi friends. In later years, Coesse became a chief and his village and later reserve were located near the present-day community of Columbia City.

When the Miamis were removed to Kansas in 1843, Coesse went with them, but refused to stay. He returned to his reserve near Columbia City. In the fall of 1853, Coesse travelled to Roanoke, Indiana, to visit his cousin, Kilsoquah, "Sun Woman" or "the setting sun." He became ill and died within two weeks. Coesse was buried near Roanoke, Indiana.

The village of Coesse, Indiana, was laid out by Peter Simmonson and honors the Miami chief.

CORNSTALK (KORN-stawk)
Settlement & stream of west Howard County (F-6)
Stream of southeast Montgomery County (H-5)

A former post office in Howard County is known as Cornstalk and a small stream is called Pete Cornstalk Creek or Pete's Run, both named after Pete Cornstalk, Ah-san-zang or Ah-son-zong meaning "sunshine," an Eel River Miami Chief of the Thorntown band. **The Preliminary History of Howard County** mentions that Pete Cornstalk lived at Indian Suck, near the southeast corner at Ervin Township. He died in 1838 and was buried north of Burlington, Indiana, on the north side of Wildcat Creek.

In Montgomery County, Cornstalk Creek, a branch of the Big Raccoon, is named for a former Indian village that was situated near the stream.

CUBA (KYU-ba)
Village in Allen County, est. 1885 (C-10)
Village in Owen County, est. 1851 (J-5)

Evidently both Indiana villages are named after the Caribbean island of Cuba of the Greater Antilles, West Indies which is derived from Cubanacan, a former tribe of the island.

The Cubanacan spoke a dialect of Arawakan language. The condensed name Cuba is believed to mean "the center or middle." Cuba also translates to mean "through" or "tank."

CUZCO (KUZ-ko)
Village in northeast Dubois County, est. 1905 (M-5)

Cuzco, Indiana, was named in the early 20th century after a city in south central Peru, capital of Apurimac Province.

Evidently the name Cuzco is Incan and means "ombligo," "navel," or "center" in reference to the old city being the heart of the Inca Empire prior to Spanish exploration.

The Indiana village probably received its unique place name from the railroad developers who were seeking something unique and memorable. The village was originally called Union Valley for its many residents were opposed to slavery during the Antebellum Period and Civil War.

DEER CREEK (DEER-kreek)
Stream in Miami, Howard, Cass & Carroll counties, (E-F-5-6-7)
Village in southeast Carroll County, (E-6)
Townships in Miami, est. 1834, Cass, est. 1829, &
Carroll, est. 1828, counties (E-F-5-6-7)

Deer Creek is a literal translation of the Miami name for the stream, passeanong, "the place of the fawn." the name was used in treaties and compounded of the word, ah-pas-syah or "a fawn."

Passeanong or Deer Creek, "place of the fawn"

According to early settlers, the white-tailed deer (Odocoileus virginianus) were found in number along the 40-mile-long stream that heads in Miami and Howard counties, flowing west and north through Cass and Carroll counties to join with the Wabash River near Delphi, Indiana.

South Fork Deer Creek and Little Deer Creek are tributaries of the stream. The Carroll County village and the three townships are named after the stream.

DELAWARE (DEL-la-ware)
Village in east central Ripley County, est. 1870 (K-10)
County in east central Indiana, est. 1827 (G-9)
Townships in Delaware, est. 1827 (G-9), Hamilton, est. 1823 (G-7), & Ripley counties, est. 1818 (K-10)

In 1610 while enroute from England to Virginia, Captain Samuel Argall discovered a bay and river which he named in honor of Thomas West, Lord de la Warr, first British Governor of Virginia. In time, the name Lord de la Warr became Delaware, a name applied to the bay, the river, and its inhabitants. The Algonquian speaking Indians of the area accepted the name of the great English "Chief."

The Delaware called themselves Lenni-Lenape or Leni-Lenape, "true men" or the "common people." They inhabited Lenpehoking "the Land of the Lenape," now the present-day mid-Atlantic seaboard states of Delaware, New Jersey, Pennsylvania and lower New York. The two distinct Delaware groups were the Munsee "people of the stony country" and the Unami "people from down river." The Lenni-Lenape were known by other tribes as Wah-pi-nach-i "people toward the rising of the sun" or E-lah-na-bah "people from the dawn," and because of their ancient lineage, they were called "grandfathers" by their Algonquian-speaking "brothers."

The Delaware were forced west and with permission from the Miami and other tribes, they began moving into southern Indiana between the White River West Fork and the Ohio River about 1770. Fourteen villages were established along the West Fork White River along with other villages primarily in east central and southeastern Indiana. According to the legend of the Walum Olum - "painted record or sticks," the Delaware had once lived on the White river about 700 to 900 years ago. Around 1818 the Delaware were forced further west into Kansas and Oklahoma where many are residents today. (see Muncie)

DOOR VILLAGE (DOOR-village)
Village in west central LaPorte County, est. 1850 (B-5)

The English translation of the French word, LaPorte, meaning "the door," is the source of the community's place name, believed to be rooted in an Algonquian word.

The word Door many have been obtained from midah-min, the Potawatomi word for maize or corn (Zea mays). According to Dunn, Door or Dormin may be a corruption of m'dah-min. Mandamin or "Indian Corn Town," was the largest and most noted Potawatomi town site in LaPorte County, located a few miles south of Door Village at Union Mills and Wellsboro, Indiana.

However, another quite important Potawatomi town was Ish-Kwan-dom, "the door," located a few miles west of Door Village at Westville, Indiana. The irregular boundaries of prairie and woodland created "a going into and coming out of" landscape, or "a narrow gap in the timber" hence "the door." LaPorte or Door Prairie was well known by the French at Ft. Bertrand, Michigan, on the St. Joseph River just north of South Bend, Indiana, and is more than likely the source for the name LaPorte.

The name may also have been derived from a Potawatomi chief who signed treaties as Me-do-min.

DRIFTWOOD (DRIFT-wud)
Stream of southeast Johnson & northeast Bartholomew counties (J-K-7-8)
Township of Jackson County, est. 1816 (L-7)

Several historic maps show the Driftwood River as the entire White River East Fork; however, it is actually a 16-mile portion from the Johnson-Bartholomew county line where the Sugar Creek and Big Blue River join, south to Columbus, Indiana. According to Indiana historian, Dunn, the Driftwood Fork of the White River was a commonly-accepted name. (see White River)

The Miami name for the river is on-gwah-sah-kah or ongivah-sah-kak meaning "driftwood." The accumulation of driftwood especially at the mouth was an important landmark in early periods and the name Driftwood would let others know what to expect below the mouth of the Big Blue River. The Delaware name gun-a-quot meaning "long" was applied.

EAST CHICAGO, NEW CHICAGO
(East, New shuh-CAW-go)
City in west Lake County, est. 1889 (A-3)
Town in northeast Lake County, est. 1907 (B-4)

Early French explorers referred to the land area at the south tip of Lake Michigan as Checago or Chicagou from possible corrupted Algonquian, Chi-cag-si-kag, She-kag-na or She-gog-ong meaning "place of the wild onion" or "place of the skunk." The Wea, a subtribe of the Miami, resided in the Chicago area at the time of French exploration. The French explorers also called the Chicago River, Riviere du Chicagou meaning "garlic creek."

Vogel believes the place name is for the wild Allium species of plants. Meadow garlic (Allium canadense), wood leek (Allium tricoccum) and nodding onion (Allium cernuum) all thrive in wooded wetland habitats along or near streams in the Chicago region.

Both northwest Indiana communities are named for Chicago, Illinois.

EEL RIVER (north) (EEL-river, north)
Stream of northeast & north central Indiana, flowing through
counties of Allen, Whitley, Wabash, Miami, & Cass,
(C-D-6-7-8-9-10)
Township in Allen County, est. 1824, (C-9-10)
Township in Cass County, est. 1829, (D-6-7)

Rising as a shallow stream north of Fort Wayne, Indiana, near Huntertown, Indiana, the Eel River flows 110 miles southwest to merge with the Wabash River at Logansport, Indiana. The Eel River Miami band, a distinct sub-tribe of the Miami nation, had several villages along its course. The Miami knew the stream as Ke-na-po-co-mo-co, Ken-na-pe-kwo-ma-kwa, or "snakefish" in reference to its winding shape and the fact the stream was a rich aquatic food source for American eel (Anguilla rostrata) which the Miami relished. Even the French called the River L'Anguille or "River of Eel."

One of the most important Miami towns along the stream during the 18th century was Kenapoco-maqua or "Old Towne." The town was situated on the river terrace on both sides of incoming Mud Creek, near Hoover, Indiana, stretching nearly three miles along the north bank of the Eel. Noted Chiefs with strong ties to Little Turtle were White Mouth and Porcupine who lived there.

Since the town was a staging ground for raids into Kentucky, Kenapoco-maqua was razed by General Wilkerson of the U.S. Army, August 7, 1791.

EEL RIVER (south) (EEL-river, south)
Stream of Putam, Clay, Owen, Greene counties (J-K-3-4)
Township in Hendricks County, est. 1824 (H-6)

Considering the headwaters begin in Boone County, the Eel River of southern and west central Indiana is over 120 miles long. The stream flows southwest to join with the White River West Fork in northern Greene County. The merger of the Walnut Fork and Mill Creek near the Owen-Clay county line form the Eel River, south.

The descriptive name is a literal translation of the Delaware schach-a-mek, schack-a-mak, sho-a-maque, or schach-a-mik meaning "straight or slippery fish" or eel (Anguilla rostrata). The stream was also known as ke-wa-be-gwinn-maig or "snow fish river." The migratory eel served as an aquatic food source for eastern Indian tribes. Shakamak State Park, near Jasonville, Indiana, is an anglicized form of the Delaware name for the eel.

ELKHART (ELK-hart)
City in central Elkhart County, est. 1832 (A-7)
County in north central Indiana, est. 1830 (A-B-7-8)
Townships in Noble and Elkhart counties, (A-B-7-8)
Streams in Noble, Lagrange & Elkhart counties (A-B-7-8-9)

Local historians report the place name was probably derived from a Shawnee Chief Elkhart or Elkheart, who came with his people into the area about 1800, rather than the elk or wapiti (Cervus elaphus)-shaped island at the mouth of the Elkhart River, now a city park. According to other legends, the Miami named the river Elkhart for the abundance of elk in the surroundings or that it was so-named for a band of Potawatomi called the Elkhart Potawatomi.

Elkhart is the literal translation of Me-sheh-weh-ou-deh-ik or Meshehwehowdehik, the Potawatomi name for the river and village located at the confluence with the St. Joseph River. The Miami name is Mishiwa-teki-sipiwi meaning "elk-heart-river."

The Elkhart River is a 38-mile-long stream in Noble and Elkhart counties, heading at the junction of its North and South branches, flowing northwest to join with the St. Joseph River in the city of Elkhart, Indiana. In addition to the North and South branches of the Elkhart River, there is also the Little Elkhart River and Little Elkhart Creek. The city, townships and county are named for the river.

ERIE (EAR-ree)
Village in central Lawrence County, est. 1867 (L-6)
Village, est. 1835 & township, est. 1835 in south Miami County, (E-7)

Originally the Erie Indians inhabited the south shore of present-day Lake Erie from western New York, and northwest Pennsylvania to northern Ohio before they were nearly destroyed by the Iroquois Confederacy in the 1650's. The tribal name Erie has been spelled Eriez, Erike, Eriga, Eriehronnon, Errieronnon and Irrironon meaning "cat nation" or "cat people" or "at the place of the panther" or "country of wild cats."

It is uncertain whether the "cat" is actually a puma or cougar or a raccoon. The French called the Iroquoian-speaking tribe, Chat Sauvage "wild cat" or Le Nation du Chat "the nation of cat" or "cat nation" referring to the raccoon. Their tribal totem was a raccoon and they painted their eye area in a similar fashion. Additional spelling variants include rhiierrhonons, riguehronons and rhiierrhonons.

The village in northeast Lawrence County is probably named after Lake Erie or Erie, Pennsylvania, the original home of some early settlers. The Wabash & Erie Canal is responsible for the Miami County place names. The canal was completed in 1837 across the southern portion of the township. The first short-lived place name for Erie Township was Black Hawk after the Sauk Chief, Ma-ka-ta-mi-ci-kiak-kiak. (see Black Hawk)

Falls of Fall Creek, Chank-tun-oon-gi or "makes a noisy place"

FALL CREEK (FALL-kreek)
Stream in northwest Henry, south Madison, southeast Hamilton, & north Marion counties, (G-7-8-9)
Townships in Henry, est. 1822, (G-9), Madison, est. 1823, (G-8), & Hamilton, est. 1823 (G-7) counties

The waterfalls at Pendleton, Indiana, account for the place name Fall Creek. The Miami knew the falls and stream as chank-tun-oon-gi or "makes a noisy place." The Delaware name, sok-pehellak, sookpehelluk or soo-sooc-pa-ha-loc translates "split water." The stream descends 25 feet in one mile near Pendleton and pioneers found it to be one of the best mill sites in Indiana. The waterfalls are within the town park and may be visited.

The stream's headwaters are in northwest Henry County. Fall

Creek flows southwest approximately 75 miles to the West Fork
White River, north of Indianapolis, Indiana. The waters of Fall
Creek fill Geist Reservoir in southeast Hamilton and northeast
Marion counties.

Based on O. H. Smith's memoirs, **The Massacre at Fall Creek** by
Jessamyn West, is a fictionalized account of the killing of peaceful
Indians by five early settlers near Pendleton, Indiana.

FLAT ROCK (FLAT-rock)
**Stream in Henry, Rush, Decatur, Shelby & Bartholomew counties
(G-H-J-7-10)**
Township in Bartholomew County, est. 1821 (K-8)

The Flat Rock River headwaters originate near Mooreland,
Henry County, Indiana, flowing south and west through a five
county course, over 90 miles before merging with the Driftwood
River at Columbus, Indiana, to become the White River East
Fork.

The Delaware called the stream pack-op-ka, puck-op-ka or
puchk-achsin probably meaning "flat rock of streambed." Perhaps
the Delaware name may have been given to the 30 water-powered
mills the settlers built, whose "flat rocks" ground grain along the
stream.

FLOWER'S CREEK (FLOWER'S-kreek)
Stream in north central Miami County (D-7)

The short stream is named in honor of Wea Captain Billy
Flowers, whose village was located at the confluence of the Eel
River, Miami County, near Chili, Indiana. His Wea name Na-go-
to-cup-wah or No-ka-me-nah, two of several spelling variants,
meant "flower." He was an important leader and warrior according
to George Winter, early 19th century artist.

The Wea, Miami and the Illini Confederacy spoke a similar
central Algonquian dialect.

GEORGETOWN (GEORGE-town)
Village in southwest Cass County, est. 1835 (E-6)

George Cicott was a son of a French-Canadian Indian trader
and Indian mother. As his father, he was an Indian trader and later
married a Indian woman, Me-shaw-ke-to-quay, a Potawatomi. Cicott lived with his in-laws in Jefferson Township,

Cass County, and was granted full Potawatomi honors.

Cicott signed the 1826 Treaty of Paradise Spring as Wabash. Indiana, turning Indian lands over to the United States. He was granted a reserve of 3.5 sections in southwestern Cass County and some land near the "Falls or Rapids of the Eel River" at Logansport, Indiana, near the confluence with the Wabash River. He settled at present-day Georgetown in 1827 to open a trading post, saw mill, and grist mill along the Wabash River and Canal. Cicott died March 29, 1833.

Four miles northwest of Georgetown along U.S. 24, 65 acre Lake Cicott and adjacent Lake Cicott village were also named in George Cicott's honor in 1868. His older brother, Zechariah or Zachriah Cicott, established a trading post at Independence, Indiana, on the north bank of the Wabash, southwest of Lafayette, Indiana. The site is now a historic Warren County Park. (see Lake Cicott)

GREENTOWN (GREEN-town)
Town in eastern Howard County, est. 1848 (F-7)

Supposedly Miami Chief Green's village was located on the site of present-day Greentown, Indiana; however, no evidence has revealed a Chief Green or an actual village. According to early surveyors there was either a natural prairie clearing in the forest or possibly a large former Indian cornfield.

HURON (HYUU-run)
Village in southwest Lawrence County, est. 1859 (M-5)

The place naming of Huron, Indiana, had nothing directly to do with the Huron Tribe. Instead sentimental settlers who emigrated from Huron County, Ohio, named the new community in memory of their former Ohio home.

The Huron lived along the shores of Georgian Bay, Ontario, Canada, until they were nearly destroyed by their Iroquoian enemies of the Six Nations in 1651. After their dispersal, they became known as Wendat, Wyandot or Wyandotte and some settled in southern Indiana in the latter 1700's. The French form of Wyandotte was Guyandot. (see Wyandotte)

The name Huron is of questionable origin. Several writers believe it is of French origin, hure for "rough" hair of the head referring to the men's styled hair ridges that resemble boar bristles. it may also mean "rough or formidable opponents." In addition, the name may be Iroquoian for a tribal totem such as hirrironon, hirron or hiron for "heron." The place name is found in several Great Lake States.

HURRICANE CREEK (HUR-ri-kane-kreek)
Stream of southwest Rush County & northwest Decatur County, tributary of Little Flatrock River, known as Little Hurricane Creek (J-9)
Stream of southeast Dubois County & northwest Perry County, tributary of the Anderson River (N-5)
Stream of southwest Spencer County, tributary of the Ohio River (O-P-4)
Stream of northwest Wells County, tributary of the Wabash River (D-9)
Stream of southwest Whitley County & southeast Kosciusko County, tribuary of the Eel River (C-D-8)
Stream of east central Johnson County, tributary of Young's Creek (J-7)

Hurricane is an English adaption of the Spanish corruption of the Amer-Indian word huracane, huracan or hurancan, possibly derived from the West Indian Carib or Arawak word, Tiano-hurakan meaning "high wind" or "god of thunder." The name was applied to several Indiana streams probably because of tropical storms that came inland from the Gulf of Mexico and carried much destruction to the area. Hurricane may also be another folk name for tornado or cyclone.

INDIAN (IN-di-an)
Indian Creek, Big & Little are found in Adams (E-10), Cass (D-6), Dubois (N-5), Floyd (N-8), Fulton (D-6), Gibson (M-3), Greene (K-5), Harrison (N-7), Knox (L-4), Marion (H-7), Martin (L-5), Monroe (K-6), Montgomery (G-4), Morgan (J-6), Owen (J-5), Pulaski (L-4), Tippecanoe (F-4) & Whitley (K-6) counties
Indian-Kentuck Creek, stream of eastern Jefferson County, (L-M-9)
Indian Heights, Kokomo, Ind. suburb, Howard County (F-7)
Indian Lake in Dekalb (B-10) & Whitley (C-8) counties
Indian Springs, village in Martin County (L-5)
Indian Village, villages in St. Joseph (A-7) & Noble (B-8) counties
Indian Creek, townships in Lawrence, est. 1818 (L-6), Monroe, est. 1818 (K-6) and Pulaski, est. 1840 (L-4) counties

The word Indian is of remote origin being from the same root stem as Hindoo and Sindhu, a name the Persians gave to the Indus River that flows from mountains of Tibet to the desert shores of the Arabian Sea. When Columbus sailed to the New World, he supposed it was India or the East Indies of Asia and called the indigenous Americans "Indios" or "Indians."

Numerous Indiana streams bear the name Indian, most likely for their former presence along these bodies of water. The townships are named for the streams that run through them. Indian-Kentuck Creek, a Jefferson County tributary of the Ohio River, adds the condensed form of Kentucky to the place name. Kentucky is of unknown Indian meaning but suggested to mean plain, meadow, head of the river, or dark and bloody ground. The latter is more generally accepted.

Indian Heights in south Kokomo, Indiana, is a coined suburban name, and probably Indian Village, north of South Bend, Indiana, is also a melodious sounding place name. Indian Village in Noble County is named for the Miami Chief Papakeechie who had a village in the area of Lake Wawasee. (see Papakeechie)

Fomerly called Short, Indiana, the place name was changed to the more enchanting Indian Springs when it was developed as a Martin County resort at the turn of the 20th century.

INDIANA (in-di-AN-a)
The 19th State admitted to the United States, December 11, 1816

The name Indiana was in use 30 years before statehood was conferred. It was first used in western Pennsylvania, Indiana County, for a tract of land obtained from the Indians in 1768 at the Treaty of Ft. Stanwix. The name may have originated with the Indiana Company, a real estate developer in Pennsylvania.

Indiana is the Latinized form of Indian meaning "Land of the Indian." The word Indian is of remote origin but is believed to be derived from Indus, the name the Persians gave to the sacred river of the Hindus of India. (see Indian) When Columbus discovered America and the West Indies, he thought it was the East Indies and India, thereby calling the inhabitants Indians or "Indios."

INDIANAPOLIS (in-di-NA-pol-lis)
Indiana's state capital & county seat of Marion County, est. 1820 (H-7)

Indianapolis is a coined word, derived from Indian and the

Greek word polis for "city." The Miami called the area Chank-tun-oon-gi or "making a noisy place" in reference to Fall Creek and the falls at Pendleton, Indiana. (see Fall Creek)

Iroquois "Greeting the French"
drawing by Steve Hudson

IROQUOIS (IR-ra-kwoy)
River in Jasper & Newton counties (D-E-3-4)
Township in Newton County, est. 1859 (D-3)

The name Iroquois was applied by the Euro-American explorers to this northwest Indiana stream before 1700. According to legend, a Potawatomi and/or Illiniwek Indian tribe subdued a war party of Iroquois on the stream during the mid-1600's. A

Potawatomi woman named Watch-e-kee or Watseka initiated the surprise attack against a raiding Iroquis war party that had earlier destroyed their village, located a few miles below Middleport, Iroquois County, Illinois. The Potawatomi called the river Pik-a-mink or Pick-a-mink meaning "full grown beavers." A tributary of the Iroquois River east of Renssalaer, Jasper County, Indiana, is today known as the Pickamink River.

Iroquois is an Algonquian word, perhaps Montagnais with French transliteration, derived from Iriakhoiw meaning "real adders or snakes." It was a name of contempt for the Six Nation League of the Iroquois who were feared by many tribes of the Northeast. The Delaware gave them the name Mingwe and the midwestern Algonquians called them Nadowa, both meaning "adders." Another source cites Iroquois as being derived from hirs, "I have said" and koul, expressing "joy or sorrow," according to the way it was pronounced.

The Iroquois call themselves Ongwanonsionni meaning "we are of the extended lodge" or Ho-de-no-sau-nee "people of the long house." They live in present-day Ontario and New York state. The Iroquois League or Confederacy consisted of Cayuga, Mohawk, Oneida, Onondaga, Seneca and Tuscarora tribes. (see Cayuga & Mohawk)

The Iroquois River heads in Jasper County and flows 48 miles west and southwest through Newton County, Indiana, to the Indiana-Illinois state line. The river flows an additional 43 miles west, north and northwest to its confluence with the Kankakee River, four miles south of Kankakee, Illinois.

JALAPA (ja-LAP-pa)
Village in northwest Grant County, est. 1849 (E-8)

Jalapa was founded by Jacob Sprecher, a farmer who sought rich fertile land. During that same year in American history, Jalapa, Mexico, had been recently captured by the Americans, defeating the Mexican Army during the Mexican-American War (1846-1848). Patriotic fever ran high and the place name was selected.

Jalapa is a Spanish word that has its roots in the Aztec word, Xalapan, literally meaning "sand by the water."

Jalapa, Indiana, is located six miles northwest of Marion, Indiana and one half mile south of the Mississenewa River.

Kankakee or Tiau-ka-keek, "low swampy land"

KANKAKEE (kang-ka-KEE)
Stream of St. Joseph, LaPorte/Starke, Porter/Jasper & Lake/Newton counties (A-B-C-3-4-5-6)
Townships in LaPorte County, est. 1833 (B-5) & Jasper County, est. 1838 (D-4)
Fish & Wildlife Area near English Lake, Indiana, Starke/LaPorte counties (B-C-5)

The most accepted source of the place name Kankakee is from the Potawatomi-Algonquian word tiau-kakeek or kia-ki-ki meaning "low swampy land or country." Now drained for agricultural farmland, the Grand Kankakee Marsh once encompassed nearly a million acres of wetlands.

Another possible, but disputed source of the name is from the Mahican or Mohican-Iroquoian word for "wolf" or "wolf place." It is believed a band of Mahican known as "wolves" from the upper Hudson River valley established villages along the Kankakee River near the headwaters in St. Joseph County after having been driven west from their eastern homeland by the Iroquois. The Miami called the river and marshlands Ma-wha-ke-ki or "wolf county."

The numerous variant spellings of Kankakee include ak-a-ki, ti-ah-ki-kink, kien-ki-ki, au-ki-ki, theas-ki-ki, aue-que-que, quin-qui-qui, the-ak-e-kee, ty-an-ki-a-kee, ti-yan-ack-aunk, ti-yan-ka-kee, ty-yan-ka-kee and theakiki.

The dredged and straightened river flows 135 miles southwest to northwest to join with the Illinois River, south of Joliet, Illinois. The Kankakee River was a strategic north-south route for the French from Canada to the Illinois Country, south to New Orleans, Louisiana. The Little Kankakee River, a tributary of the Kankakee River, flows south and east to join in southeast LaPorte County, Indiana.

KAPPA (KAP-pa)
Village in northwest Howard County, est. 1886 (F-6)

Some authorities believe the name Kappa is a corruption of Quapaw, an early southwest Siouan-speaking tribe that was present in Indiana along the lower Wabash River valley until the early 16th century. Quapaw is from Ugakhpa or Capaha meaning "downstream people."

The Quapaw were later found on the west bank of the Mississippi River, north of the mouth of the Arkansas River when DeSoto encountered the tribe (1539-43). They became known as the Arkansea or Arkansas.

KEWANNA (kee-WAA-na)
Town in west central Fulton County, est. 1845 (D-6)

Kewanna is named for the Potawatomi War Chief Kee-way-nay (1790's?-1840's?) who lived along the banks of Ke-na-po-co-mo-co or Eel River (north) and later at Lake Kee-waw-nay, Kee-wa-knay or Lake Bruce. According to today's literature, his name is spelled a variety of ways: Kee-wa-nee, Kewaunay, Kee-wee-naw, Kewaunee, Kewaune, Ke-won-nee and Ki-wa-na. Most documented sources agree the name probably means, "prairie chicken or hen," although "lost" and "to

Kee-waw-nay or "prairie chicken"
painting by Ronald Prilliman
based on the original by George Winter

go around" also appear as possible definition, along with "wild duck." The prairie chicken (Tympanuchus cupido) was once common in prairies and woodland clearings in Indiana, but it is now confined to isolated birds in Jasper and Newton counties.

The closely-related Ojibway word, Kewaunee, Kewenaw, or Keweena, a corruption of Ka-ki-we-o-nan, refers to a canoe portage across a peninsula or point of land. According to Vogel, Kewanee, Illinois, may possibly be named after the same northern Indiana Potawatomi War Chief. Ke-wah-ni, a Miami word, means "nose."

Chief Kee-waw-nay was present at the signing of several land treaties between the Potawatomi and the United States. He fought together with the Shawnee Tecumseh during the War of 1812. Pioneer artist, George Winter, painted and recorded a personal description of the tribal leader in his journal during a treaty negotiation at present-day Lake Bruce, six miles northwest of Kewanna in 1837.

Due to his looming presence, the settlers named the body of water, Lake Kee-waw-nay, until the 1840's when the locals renamed it Lake Bruce. During the same time, nearby Pleasant Grove was experiencing place name confusion with other like-named Hoosier communities; therefore, the U.S. Postal Service changed the name to Kewanna.

Local historian, Bromley Smith, summed up the place name history as thus:

> "Thus the former village of Pleasant Grove
> alias Pinhook, became the second incorporated
> town in Fulton County, its name agreeing
> with that of the post office-Kewanna, the
> beautiful town of "Prairie Chicken."

Kee-waw-nay and his tribal band went west to Kansas in 1837.

KICKAPOO CREEK (KICK-ka-puu-kreek)
Stream in northwest Warren County (F-3-4)

The Kickapoo tribal name is derived from Kiikaapoa, Kiwigapawa or Kiwegapaw, a name whose meaning is unknown, but is often cited as, "those who move about" or "he moves about, standing now here, now there" in reference to the tribes nomadic existence or wanderings.

Once entering Indiana, the Kickapoo settled on the banks of the Wabash and Vermillion rivers. Kickapoo are allies of the

Illinois Prairie Potawatomi or Mascoutens and established a village with them on the north side of the Wabash River opposite Wea Town near Fort Ouiatenon, downstream from present-day Lafayette, Indiana, that was destroyed around 1790.

Later, the Kickapoo joined with the Miami to destroy the American advance and were numerous at the Battle of Tippecanoe in 1811. The last of the Kickapoo land at the Vermillion and Wabash confluence was ceded in 1809. Never large in numbers in Indiana, the remaining Kickapoo ceded their lands and moved west, some as far as Mexico.

KILLBUCK CREEK (KIL-buck-kreek)
Stream in west central Delaware & east central Madison counties (F-G-8-9)

Killbuck Creek is named for Delaware Chief Kelelamand or "big cat" better known as Charles Henry Killbuck (late 1700's - early 1800's). Killbuck was the son of William Henry Killbuck, who after the death of White Eyes or Koquethagechton in 1778, was temporarily the First Chief of the Delawares.

Killbuck's village or Buck's Town was located on a high bluff east of the White River west fork, one mile northwest of the town of Chesterfield, Indiana. Killbuck was converted by the Moravian Christian missionaries who worked among the White River Delawares. His name appears on treaties signed in Ft. Wayne, Indiana, 1809 and St. Marys, Ohio, 1818.

The headwaters begin near Royerton, Indiana, in west central Delaware County and flow southwest to the White River's west fork near Anderson, Indiana. Two tributaries are both named Little Buck Creek.

KLONDIKE, KLONDYKE (KLON-dike)
Village in northwest Tippecanoe County, est. 1897 (F-4)
Village in west central Parke County, est. 1907 (H-3)
Village in southeast Vermillion County, est. 1902 (H-3)

All three west central Indiana communities were directly or indirectly named for the region in the Yukon Territory of Canada that was famous for the Gold Rush of 1897-1899. The villages in Tippecanoe and Parke counties were apparently named in the excitement of the Yukon gold rush. The Vermillion County Klondyke is named for the local coal mines that operated about the same time as the Yukon Gold Rush.

Klondike or Klondyke is an English corruption of an Athapascan Kutchin Indian word, tron-duik or thron-diuck meaning "hammer water" or "fish river," in reference to the Klandark River, a tributary of the Yukon River. The stream is rich with salmon and nets were supported with stakes "hammered" into the shoreline, hence the name.

KOKOMO (KO-ko-mo)
City in central Howard County, est. 1844 (F-7)
Creek in south central Howard County (F-7)

Kokomo, the county seat for Howard County, is a place name familiar to most Hoosiers. The city's name is derived from the Miami War Chief Ko-ko-ma, Ko-kah-mah, Ko-ka-mah, or Ko-ko-mo-ko (1775?-1841?). His Miami name has several interpretations including "the diver," "he goes under," "black walnut," "old woman," "young grandmother," "she bear," "bear chief," or "wise like an owl." Ko-ko-ma was the son of Chief Richardville and Tah-kum-wah.

Kokomo, Miami Chief
painting by Ida Gordon

Most of the Miami population of Howard County lived in Chief Ko-ko-ma's village located on the banks of the Wildcat Creek near the center of Washington Street. There is a city memorial for Kokomo and early settlers of Howard County at the end of Purdum Street in Kokomo, Indiana.

Kokomo Creek, is a short stream of south central Howard County, that flows west to join Wildcat Creek at Kokomo, Indiana. The headwaters are near Hemlock and Center, Indiana.

LACROSSE (la-KROS)
Town in southwest LaPorte County, est. 1868 (C-5)

LaCrosse is a town with a French name of questionable origin. Either the Indians played the game lacrosse in the area, borrowed the name from another location, or the name was wrongly applied to mean "a crossing." LaCrosse, founded in 1868, was a crossing for four railroads and could possibly refer to the location as a crossroads.

However, reports mention the early French explorers watched the competitive game played in the Kankakee Valley area by Native Americans. The French called it lacrosse meaning, "hooked stick" or "a cross," since the playing stick the Indians used resemble a Catholic bishop's cross or crozier. The Algonquian name for the game of skill and strengh was baggataway, baggatiway or pan-kee-to-way.

LAFONTAINE (la-FOUN-ton)
Town in southeast Wabash County, est. 1862 (E-8)

Francois or Francis LaFontaine Jr. (1810-1847) was a Miami Chief whose father was French and his mother Miami. His French surname means, "the fountain" or "source." The chief's Miami name was To-pe-ah or To-pi-a, said to be a contraction of the Potawatomi personal name Toppinabin, meaning "frost on the bushes."

LaFontaine was born near Ft. Wayne at the time of Miami decline (C.1810). He married Chief Richardville's daughter, Po-con-go-quah, at age 21. His interest in the well-being of the Miami Nation elected him chief after the death of Chief Jean Baptiste Richardville or Pin-jeh-wah. (see Russiaville)

Chief LaFontaine resided and owned a trading post near the Forks of the Wabash, two miles west of Huntington, Indiana. His home at the forks also served as tribal headquarters. LaFontaine traveled west with the tribe in 1846, but returned the following year to Indiana. He died in Lafayette, Indiana, and was buried in Mt. Calvary Cemetery in north Huntington.

In 1880 the town of Ashland, Indiana, Wabash County was renamed LaFontaine in the chief's honor.

LAGRO (LAY-grow)
Town est. 1829 & Township est. 1835, east central Wabash County (D-8)
Creek in Lagro Township, Wabash County (D-8)

Lagro is a corruption for the French nickname of the Miami-French Chief, Le Gros (1770's?-1831) or "big body" or "the great" in reference to his obese size. Largo's Miami name was O-sah-la-mo-nee or Ah-sah-mo-nee meaning "bloodroot" or "yellow paint" in reference to a native wildflower (Sanguinaria canadensis) which yields a yellow dye.

Le Gros Town or Osahlamonee's Town occupied the north bank of the Wabash River at the confluence with the Salamonie River. Prior to American settlement, the town was a trade center for the French traders and Indians. Chief Le Gros willed his land acquired by the treaties of 1818 and 1826 to General John Tipton who organized the town, naming it in Le Gros' honor.

"Couple on Horseback by Lake," possibly Lake Cicott
painting by George Winter

LAKE CICOTT (lake-SAI-kut)
Village & 65 acre lake in southwest Cass County, est. 1868 (E-6)

The village of Lake Cicott was named after the spring-fed lake that was named in honor of George Cicott, French Indian trader who was married to Me-shaw-ke-to-quay, a Potawatomi woman. During the mid-19th century the water body was also called George Town Lake, in honor of Cicott (see Georgetown)

LAKE LENAPE (lake-la-NAA-pee)
Lake at Shakamak State Park, northwest Greene County (K-3-4)

The 36-acre recreational lake was created from surface coal mining as was nearby 56-acre Shakamak Lake, both within the boundries of Shakamak State Park, two miles northwest of Jasonville, Indiana, in Wright Township.

The lake's name Lenape is derived from the Delaware name for its people, Lenni Lenape meaning "the common people" or "true men." (see Delaware)

"The Monster of Lake Manitou"
drawing by Angie Neidlinger

LAKE MANITOU (lake-MAN-a-tow)
713 acre lake southeast of Rochester, central Fulton County (D-7)

The scenic lake received its place name from an ancient Potawatomi or Chippewa legend. According to the legend, as many as three evil "Matchi" monster fish came overland from Lake Michigan to the lake, whirling like a tornado and creating much destruction. The terrible spirit or spirits lived in the lake, devouring all wildlife who lived there and those who came to visit. The Indians would not canoe upon its waters or eat fish from the lake. The neighboring tribes prayed to the Good Spirit, Gitchi Kitchi Maneto, or Maito, to destroy the monsters and their prayers were answered. Grateful to the good spirit, they named the lake in his honor, Man-i-toe.

The French word manitou or manitau is derived from the Algonquian word ma-ne-to or manito for "spirit." The Miami name for spirit is mah-nat-o-wah. A captured buffalo fish (Ictiobus cyprinellus) measured up to nine feet long and is thought to be the "monster" of Lake Manitou. Early settlers called the lake. Devil's Lake.

The location at the lake outlet is known as Potawatomi Mills. In 1827, a grist mill was constructed by the U.S. Government to grind corn for the Potawatomi under terms of a 1826 treaty, which later fell into non-use after their removal in 1838.

LOGANSPORT (LOW-gans-port)
County seat of Cass County, est. 1828 (E-6)

Situated at the confluence of the Eel River or Ke-na-po-co-mo-co, "snakefish," and the Wabash River, Wah-bah-shik-ki, "pure bright water," is the city of Logansport, originally Logan's Port. The river "City of Bridges," is named for a nephew of Tecumseh (1782-1812) whose adopted personal American name is John Logan. His Shawnee name was Spemica Lawba or Spamagelake, meaning "high horn." (1782-1812).

Spemica Lawba was taken captive when he was four years old in 1786 by the American army. He was raised in Kentucky by General Benjamin Logan and given the family name. When his Shawnee blood father died, his adopted father allowed him to return to his people in Ohio to serve as chief, but his loyalties were with the American forces in the War of 1812. He served with William Henry Harrison and his "Yellow Jackets" at the November 1811, Battle of Tippecanoe, later obtaining the rank of Captain. The following year while serving with the U.S. army he was killed by hostile Potawatomi and a British Captain led by Chief Winamac near Fort Wayne, and was buried at Defiance, Ohio.

Rather than flipping a coin or voting, the city fathers, who were former soldiers, who knew and respected Captain Logan, held a muzzle shooting contest to select names for the new community. Col. John B. Duret, who won the right to name the town, named it in honor of Capt. Logan.

MACONAQUAH (ma-KAA-na-kwa)
High school in south Miami County (E-7)
City park in south Peru, Indiana (E-7)

The school and park are named in honor of Maconaquah, Maconsquah, Maconsqah, Ma-co-za-quah, or Mah-con-es-quah meaning "little bear woman" also known as Frances Slocum, "White Rose of the Miami" (1773-1847). At five years old, she was kidnapped by Delaware Indians in 1778 from her Pennsylvania Quaker home in the Wyoming Valley, near Wilkes-Barre.

During the next 60 years, she married twice, first to Delaware brave, Little Turtle, and later a Miami, She-pa-can-wah, Shepoconah or She-apn-can-ah, "deaf war chief." Maconaquah gave birth to four children, two boys who died young and two girls name Kick-ke-ne-che-quah or "cut finger" and O-sah-shin-quah or "yellow leaf." She is buried adjacent to her second husband in Wabash County at the Frances Slocum State Recreation Area, Mississinewa Lake Reservoir.

MAJENICA (ma-JEN-a-ka)
Village, est. 1852 & stream in south central Huntington County (E-8-9)

Majenica commemorates the Miami Chief Man-ji-ni-kia or "big body," "big frame," "big leg," or the "big Miami" in reference to his large body size. Local 19th century journalist, Thad Butler wrote Majenica's village was on the south side of the Wabash River at the settlement of Belden, three miles east of Andrews, Indiana, on the Wabash-Huntington county line. His later reserve was in the same area as the present-day community which is located on the south bank of Majenica Creek that flows to the Salamonie River. According to McClure, an Indian trader, his good will was courted, hated and feared.

Additional spelling variants of his name include Mon-je-ni-kyah, Man-je-ne-ki-ah, Minjenickeaw, Metchenchqua, Met-chin-e-qua, Magenca, Magincea, Me-chin-e-ca, and Majenica. He died prior to the removal of his band to the west.

MANHATTAN (man-HAT-ton)
Village in southwest Putnam County, est. 1829 (J-5)

This Indiana community's place name is a transfer from Manhattan Island, New York. The Indian origin of the name is uncertain.

The Manhattans were Algonquian and lived in the present-day New York City area and Hudson Valley. They were allied with the Delaware. The name probably means "island," "hill island," "island of hills" or "island village." Additional spelling variants include Man-a-hat-ta-ni, Manahtans, Mannahata, Mannahatin, Monahtanuk, Manhutton, Manhattos, Munatthans, Manahatas, Menatey, and Manatte.

MAUMEE (MAW-mee)
Township & stream in Allen County (C-10-11)
Settlement in northwest Jackson County (L-6)

The Maumee River or "Miami of the Lake," is a tributary of Lake Erie. The stream is formed from the confluence of the St. Marys and St. Joseph rivers at present-day Ft. Wayne, Indiana, flowing 100 miles to Maumee Bay at Lake Erie, northwest of Toledo, Ohio. The name is a corruption of the Miami tribal name Me-ah-me or Meame meaning "friends" or "all beavers." (see Miami)

Kekionga, now Ft. Wayne, became the Miami's primary town in the late 1700's. The Maumee or Mawmee was formerly known as the "river of the Miamis" and the Ottawa River. An Ottawa subtribe called Kiskakons or "clipped hair" lived along the river prior to Miami occupation, hence Kekionga. Kekionga is also reputed to mean "blackberry patch."

Shoreline of Lake Maxinkuckee or "big stone country"

MAXINKUCKEE (MACK-son-kuck-kee)
Lake at Culver, Indiana, Marshall County (C-6)
Village on east side of Lake Maxinkuckee, est. 1837 (C-6)

One of the largest natural lakes in Indiana, Maxinkuckee is an alteration of the Potawatomi name, Mog-sin-kee-ki also spelled Mexancukke, Mux-in-kuck-key or Mux-see-cuck-ee meaning, "big stone country." The glacial morraines of the Wisconsin Age left behind elevated ridges, kames and rock bars of till rock, around and in the 1,854 acre scenic lake.

Additional interpretations for Maxinkuckee include, "clear water," "diamond lake," "beautiful or charming water," "big medicine" and "moccasin lake."

Menominee Monument, Potawatomi Chief, "wild rice eater"

MENOMINEE STATE PUBLIC FISHING AREA
(me-na-MEE-nee)
State Fish & Wildlife Property along the Tippecanoe River in north central Fulton County (C-7)

MENOMINEE STATE WETLAND CONSERVATION AREA
State Fish & Wildlife Area in central & west central Marshal County (B-C-7)

These two Fish and Wildlife properties in north central Indiana are named after Chief Menominee or Me-no-mi-nee (1791?-1841), a Potawatomi whose personal name means "wild rice-people or eater." The name is derived from the Ojibwa word, Manomini. Menominee's village was located at Twin Lakes in south central Marshall County and was the largest and most important Potawatomi village in the area.

Menominee refused to sign any treaties selling his lands to the United States, but it was signed away by other chiefs at a treaty held on the Tippecanoe River, Chippewanung Village, Fulton County, in 1836. Menominee's and his Christian band of 859 Potawatomi were forcibly removed to Kansas in 1838. The forced march is known as the Trail of Death. He died April 15, 1941, age 50, at St. Mary's Mission at Sugar Creek, Kansas, according to Catholic records.

A monument to Chief Menominee is located near Twin Lakes on South Peach Road, 6.5 miles southwest of Plymouth, Indiana.

METAMORA (me-ta-MOW-ra)
Village in northwest Franklin County, est. 1838 (J-10)

The Indiana community is named after the title and leading character actor in John Augustus Stone's most important play, "Metamora: Last of the Wampanoags" (1829), a significant first-of-its-kind aboriginal drama with mixed Wampanoags-Anglo dialect.

Metamora is the Latinized form of Me-ta-com-et, Metacom, or Pometacom, "strong spirit or heart." Me-ta-com-et was the youngest son of Chief Massasoit, better known as King Philip in United States history (1638?-1676). Me-ta-com-et succeeded his brother, Wamsutta or Alexander, as sachem of the Wampanoag Indians, an Algonquian-speaking people of the lower Hudson Valley and central New England that numbered over 1,600 people in the early 1600's. Today they are found in smaller numbers living in Massachusetts and Rhode Island.

Me-ta-com-et or Metamora defended his people and lands against the New England colonists in an uprising known as King Philip's War (1675-1676); a series of massacres in the villages of interior Rhode Island and Connecticut. Nearing capture, Me-ta-com-et took refuge near Bristol, Rhode Island, where he was killed August 12, 1676.

According to local traditions of the residents of Metamora, Indiana, there is mention of a Metamoris, a Delaware Chief, who lived in the Wapinepay or Whitewater River valley. Supposedly, Metamoris accompanied Tecumseh in his travels to unite the tribes into a confederacy to halt Euro-American advancement.

METEA (MEE-tee-a)
Village in north central Cass County, est. 1853 (D-6)

Metea, Metawa, Me-te-ah, Meteah, or Mi-ti-a (1760?-1827) was one of the better-known Potawatomi Chiefs who lived in the village of Mus-kwau-asep-eo-tan, Muskwawasipiotan, or Mes-kwah-wah-se-pe meaning "red cedar stream village" or "cedar creek town," located twelve miles north of Fort Wayne, Indiana, at the confluence of Cedar Creek and the Saint Joseph River, which was called Ko-chis-oh-se-pe or "bean river" by the Miami. Metea roamed Cass County, but never considered it home. The village is probably named for a camp Metea had there for an unknown length of time.

Most written accounts consider Metea to mean "kiss me" but

it could be from Metawa, "he sulks" or "prophet" or "priest" from Potawatomi meda or meta. The noted chief was born at the time of the American Revolution and was known for his oratory in council, knowledge of the tradition of his people and his bravery in battle. He participated in the War of 1812. Metea attended important conferences with the Americans and signed treaties, ending Potawatomi hostilities. He died of poisoning at Fort Wayne in

Metea, Potawatomi Chief
painting by
Thomas L. McKenney & James Hall

1827 and was buried near the Saint Mary's River. An Allen County Park is named in his honor.

METOCINAH, METACINAH CREEK
ALSO SPELLED JOCINAH, JOSINA CREEK
(me-tow-SEE-naa or jo-SEE-naa-kreek)
Stream in northeast Grant County & southeast Miami County
(E-8)

Metocinah or Jocinah Creek is derived from the Miami Chief Metocenyah or Metocena, often called Tosanyah or Too-san-ea, meaning "the living" or "Indian," "the father of Meshingomesia", or "burr oak tree." The chief's village was located near the creek's mouth at the Mississinewa River, southwest of LaFontaine, Indiana, near the site of the 1812 Battle of the Mississinewa, the last Miami-American armed conflict.

The Grant County south branch section of the stream usually appears on maps and other literature as Jocinah Creek while the north branch is Metocinah Creek.

MEXICO (MECK-si-ko)
Village in west central Miami County, est. 1834 (E-7)

Twelve years before the Mexican-American War, this north central Indiana community commemorated the independence of Mexico from Spain by naming itself for the new nation.

The place name is derived from the Nahuatl language of the Aztecs, the most powerful of all the pre-Columbian Indian tribes. Nomadic at first, the Aztecs organized early in the 12th century, led by their war-god king, Mexitli, the origin of the name Mexico, meaning "place of the moon," "center of the moon" or "habitation of the god of war." The historic Aztec temple of Mexitl is located in present-day Mexico City, Mexico.

MIAMI (my-AM-i)
County in north central Indiana, est. 1834 (D-E-7)
Townships in Miami, est. 1834 (D-E-7) & Cass counties, est. 1829 (D-6)
Village in southwest Miami County, est. 1849 (E-7)
High school in north Miami County (D-7)

"Vision Quest," Miami Brave
drawing by Angie Neidlinger

Migrating southeastward from Wisconsin and Michigan, the Miami was the dominant tribe occupying Indiana during the 18th century. The Miami divided into several bands that inhabited permanent villages along the Wabash River and Fort Wayne, Indiana (see Wea & Eel River, north).

The origin of the Algonquian tribal name is not clear, but is believed to be a name given to them by another tribe, possibly the Ojibwa. The Ojibwa name for Miami is Oumaumeg meaning "people of the peninsula," possibly in reference to the Door Peninsula at Green Bay, Wisconsin. The Miami's closest allies, the Delaware called them We-mi-a-mik or Wemiamick meaning "all friends" or "beavers." The French name Oumiamiouek or Oumiamiak was similar to the Delaware. Monami is "my friend" in French. The English name for the Miami was Twightwees, "the cry of the crane." Another possible source is the Miami word meeneea or meearmee meaning "pigeon."

Just as there are many explanations for the name origin, so are there numerous ways Miami is spelled. One historic source lists 86 spelling variations and alternate names for the tribe.

Several hundred Miami families live in Miami County today and the Miami Nation of Indians of the State of Indiana is headquartered in Peru, Indiana. They call themselves, Wa-ya-ta-no-ke or Me-a-me-a-ga meaning "nation born from edding water."

MICHIGAN (MI-shi-gan)
One of the five Great Lakes of North America (22,400 sq. miles), northwest Indiana (A-B-3-4-5)
Town, city, est. 1831 and township, est. 1832 in LaPorte County, (A-B-5)
Township & town, est. 1830, in Clinton County, (F-6)

The name Michigan is derived from the Ojibwa word, Mi-shi-sa-gie-gan or Mi-ski-sa-gie-gan meaning the "great lake or water." The Miami called the lake, Mischigonong or "great lake." The Potawatomi name is from Mitchasagaigau, also meaning "great lake."

Nearly 220 miles of Lake Michigan is located within Indiana's boundaries. Indiana communities with Lake Michigan place names include Michiana Shores, Michigan City and Michigantown.

The Michigan Road/U.S. 421 runs from Madison, Indiana, on the Ohio River to Lake Michigan. Many towns including South Bend have their main street named Michigan Street, because it was formerly the Michigan Road. Also, the regional area of Michiana, and Lake County in northwest Indiana derive their name from Lake Michigan.

Mi-shi-sa-gie-gan or "great water," Lake Michigan

MINNEHAHA (min-ne-HA-ha)
State Fish & Wildlife area, eastern Sullivan County (K-3)

The former 12,500 acre strip mine pits were reclaimed by the Indiana Department of Natural Resources, Division of Fish and Wildlife during the 1980's. The area is named after Longfellow's heroine in his epic poem, **Song of Hiawatha.**

The corrupted name is derived from the Teton Sioux dialect of the Dakota people, Minne-rara meaning "laughing waters," "water laughter," "falling waters" or "waterfall." Minnehaha is also the name of a noted waterfall near Fort Snelling, Minnesota.

MISHAWAKA (mi-sha-WAWK-ka)
City in northeast St. Joseph County, est. 1833 (A-7)

The place name Mishawaka is derived from a corrupted Shawnee or Potawatomi word, M'Shehwahkeek or M'seh-wah-kei-ki possibly meaning "swift flowing water," "heavy timberlands," "thick woods," or "place of dead trees." Local historians believe the name identifies the swift rapids in the river where an Indian village by the same name was located. Several authorities report the name means, "place of dead trees" in regard to the practice of girdling trees to clear an area or possibly a tornado windfall.

According to local folklore, the city was named after a Shawnee Indian princess, M-Shehwahkeek "swift water," the daughter

Chief Elkhart. The fictitious legend and characters were born at Three Rivers, Michigan, where the Shawnee battled the Potawatomi in the early 1800's.

The romantic, but untrue story tells that while Chief Elkhart was severely wounded in battle, his daughter M'Shehwahkeek rallied the Shawnee but was soon captured by the Potawatomi. M'Shehwahkeek fell in love with a young American scout named Dead Shot. Gray Wolf, a Shawnee sub-chief, also wanted her love, and fought with Dead Shot, stabbing M'Shehwahkeek before his death. Dead Shot nursed her back to health. The couple married and lived along the St. Joseph River. Sometime during the early 20th century the citizens of Mishawaka adopted the legend of M'Shehwahkeek. Local civic organizations went as far as to establish a memorial plaque dedicated to "Princess Mishawaka" in 1932 in Lincoln Park near the St. Joseph River. (see Elkhart)

Mississinewa River or Na-ma-tei-sin-wi "much fall in the water"
Seven Pillars of the Mississinewa

MISSISSINEWA (mi-si-SI-na-waa)
River & reservoir lake in Delaware, Grant, Wabash & Miami counties (E-F-7-10)

The Mississinewa River's headwaters are in northwestern Ohio, a few miles south of the Wabash River's origins. The stream flows northwest about 100 miles before joining the Wabash River in Miami County, Indiana. Statewide the Mississinewa is one of the swiftest streams. The 14,000 acre reservoir lake, situated seven miles southeast of Peru, Indiana, is named in honor of the river.

The river was named by the Miami who call it, Na-ma-tei-sin-wi, Na-mah-chis-sin-wa and Mas-pis-sin-e-way meaning, "much fall in the water," "falling water" or "it slopes or slants" in regard to its many rapids.

Mississenawa has been spelled Mas-sis-sin-e-way, Massis-sinoue, Massassinawa, Missasinua, Mississinway, and Mississineway. Former Miami villages along the stream include Wahshahshie, Meskingomeshia, and Metosanyah. The last Miami-American armed conflict was the 1812 Battle of the Mississinewa, near Metosanyah's village, south of LaFontaine, Indiana. The Seven Pillars of the Mississinewa near Peru, Indiana, are culturally significant to the Miami. These pillars and cornices are eroded limestone that form the entrances to shallow caves.

MIXSAWBAH (mik-SAW-baa)
State Fish Hatchery in southeast LaPorte County, est. 1974 (B-6)

Mixsawbah or Macsawbee was a Potawatomi Indian chief who lived in the Kankakee River area during the early 1800's. He was present at a parley on the Tippecanoe River, signing a treaty with the U.S. government in 1832 that ceded all Potawatomi land holdings in Indiana, Illinois, and Michigan. Mixsawbah is of uncertain meaning.

The naming of the state facility was suggested by LaPorte County historian, Gene McDonald, whose ancestors were hunters and trappers during the early 1800's. The coldwater trout and salmon fish hatchery is located at the Kingsbury State Fish & Game Area, County Road 673.

MODOC (MOW-dock)
Town in southwest Randolph County, est. 1882 (G-10)

Modoc, Indiana, commemorates the Modoc Indians, a Lutuamian-speaking tribe of southern Oregon and northern California who held off U.S. troops from 1872-1873 in what is historically known as "The Modoc War."

The anglicized name is the corrupted form of Modokni or Moatokni meaning "southern people," a name given by their neighbors to the north of the Mococ, the Klamath. The name's linguistic stock is Shapwailutan.

MOHAWK(MOW-hawk)
Village in northwest Hancock County, est. 1883 (H-8)

The Mohawk are one of six nations of the Iroquois Confederation occupying the region along New York's eastern border, including the Mohawk Valley and the Hudson River. The Indiana place name is for the tribe, but no one is certain of the origin of the Mohawk name.

The tribal name Mohawk is believed to have been given to the "keepers of the eastern door" by an enemy Algonquian tribe, possibly Narrassanet. Mohawk is derived from Maugwawogs, Mauquawog, Mohowauuck, Maqua, Mohowaugsuck meaning "man eaters," "cannibals" or possibly "bear."

The Mohawk call themselves Ga-ne-ga-o-no, Kaniengehaga, or Canniengas meaning "people of the place of flint." (see Iroquois, Cayuga)

MONGO (MONG-go)
Village in northeast Lagrange County, est. 1840 (A-9)

When the community was platted, the place name was Mongoquinong, a Potawatomi word meaning "big" or "old squaw prairie." A large Potawatomi village by that name was located ten miles downstream on the Pigeon River or Wahbememe, ("White Pigeon,") where the village of Howe is located today.

The village had several thousand inhabitants, but by 1828 the tribal center had only 30 wigwams scattered along the Pigeon River. (see Pigeon River)

Highway Signs at and near Monon, Indiana

MONON (MOW-non)
Town, est. 1838, & township est. 1834, in northwest White County (D-5)
Streams in west Pulaski and central White counties (C-D-E-5-6)

The town of Monon was named for the township that borrowed

its name from two streams that cross the area. The small stream, flowing on the south side of Monon, Indiana, was called Monong by the Potawatomi, and the larger stream, located a few miles east of town, was called Metamonong meaning "to carry or tote."

A local historian believes the Potawatomi name Monong means "swift running" and Metamonong means "big swift running." The headwaters of Big Monon Creek were known as Metamonong Swamp, now drained. The place name Monon is also accredited to the Monon Railroad, Indiana's beloved "Hoosier Line" that offered over a century of passenger service to the state.

The Big and Little Monon Creeks drain western Pulaski and central White counties, flowing south and east to join with Lake Shafer and the Tippecanoe River.

MONOQUET (ma-NOCK-kwot)
Village in central Koscuisko County, est. 1834 (C-7)

Monoquet or Menoquet (1790's?-1830's?) "banked cloud" was a Potawatomi chief and warrior whose village and reserve were located three miles north of present-day Warsaw, Indiana, where State Road 15 crosses the Tippecanoe River, and the site of the present-day village.

**Me-no-quet or "banked cloud,"
Potawatomi Chief**
painting by James Otto Lewis

Monoquet, often spelled Menoquet, participated in the Battle of Tippecanoe and the War of 1812 under Tecumseh. Monoquet died of lung fever, although members of his tribe at the time thought the chief was killed by a young woman from Chief White Pigeon's tribe. Monoquet was buried on the banks of the Tippecanoe near the village of Monoquet.

Variant spellings of his name include Menucquet, Menukquet, and Manoquett.

MONTEZUMA (mon-ta-ZUU-ma)
Town in west central Parke County, est. 1849 (H-3)

Montezuma is the Spanish name of the Aztec emperor Moc-tezuma Ilhuicamina, the great grandson of Montezuma I (1440-1469). Montezuma II (1466-1520) reigned over the present-day Mexico City and southern Mexico area for 40 years. The Spanish-led invasion by Hernando Cortes in 1519 ended his rule.

The Aztecs believed Cortes was Quetzalcoatl, the "white cloud" who had sailed away years before, but promised to return. Montezuma II was killed by a stone thrown either by the Spaniards or his own people during the Aztec overthrow.

Montezuma may mean "master of the heavens, like an eagle" or the "angry one who shoots arrows in the sky." Spelling variants of Montezuma include Motezuma, Moctezuma, Motenczoma, Motechuhzoma, Moteuczomatzen and Mon-quau-zo-ma.

The Indiana village was named one year after the Mexican-American War (1846-1848), probably in honor of American victory.

MUNCIE (MUN-see)
City & county seat of Delaware County, est. 1818 (G-9)
Creek tributary of White River West Fork, Delaware County (G-9)
Lake, south central Noble County (C-9)

Muncie is a corruption of Minsi, Min-si, Min-thi-u or Min-asin-ink meaning "people of the stony country," "at the place where the stones are gathered together," "the great stone," or "mountaineers". One of two tribal divisions of the Lenni-Lenape or Delaware, the Munsee originated in the lower east Hudson River Valley of New York and the upper Delaware River down to the confluence with the Lehigh River in New Jersey and Pennsylvania. The Munsee subdivisions include the Minisink, Warar-sinks, Katskills, and Waoranecks.

The totem of the Munsee is the Tookseat of Wolf clan. The Munsee creation myth is that their ancestors and all animals once lived inside the earth. One day a wolf chased a deer and discovered the way to the earth's surface. The wolf guided the people from the underground to the sunlit lands above. The Munsee were called "loups" or "wolves" by the French.

Forced west, the Munsee Delaware made several villages along

"Appeal to the Great Spirit"
north bank of the White River, Muncie, Indiana

the White River West Fork including the present-day site of Muncie, Indiana, along Minnetrista (Sioux, "crooked water") Boulevard. Munseetown was also called Tatapachski, Tatapaksit, or Telipokshy Town "twisting vine," after a Christian chief of the White River Delaware who was executed for witchcraft by Tenskwatawa, "The Prophet" or "the open door" in 1806. Muncie was also called Outainink.

The Delaware at St. Marys, Ohio, ceded all their lands in Indiana to the United States in 1818, they moved further west to Kansas and eventually Oklahoma. (see Delaware)

MUSCATATUCK RIVER (mus-KAT-ta-tuck river)
Stream of southeast Indiana (L-7-8-9)

The Muscatatuck River drains over 1,000 miles of Jefferson, Jennings, Scott, Washington and Jackson counties, a major tributary of the White River East Fork or the Driftwood Fork. The main stream of the Muscatatuck begins in northwest Jefferson County near Paris Crossing, Indiana, heading at the junction of Big Creek and Graham Creek. The river flows 53 miles westward to the White River East Fork south of Medora, Indiana.

The descriptive name is a corruption of the Delaware word for the stream, Mosch-ach-hit-tuck or Mesh-caque-tuck, meaning "stream flowing through swampy land," "pond river" or "clear river" from its many quiet pools in low water.

MUSKELONGE LAKE (MUSK-lounge-lake)
Lake in south central Kosciusko County (C-8)

Muskelonge Lake is a 24-acre marl-bottom lake located five miles south of Warsaw, the county seat. Muskelonge is derived from maskinonge, an Ojibwa word for "the great pike," muskellunge (Esox masquinongy), the largest member of the Pike family. State fishery biologists report that it is unlikely any muskellunge are native to the lake, so the place name is considered wishful thinking.

The name also appears as Muskelunge on some state maps. The lake is drained by Walnut Creek that flows north to join with the Tippecanoe River.

NAPPANEE (nap-pa-NEE)
City in southwest Elkhart County, est. 1874 (B-7)

Nappanee, Indiana, is named after Napanee, south Ontario, Canada. Early settlers George and Henry Eby, who formerly resided in Napanee, Ontario, suggested the name of their newly-adopted community, adding another "p," but some historians cite Daniel Metzler with the honor of the place name.

The original meaning is lost, but supposedly it is derived from the Missisauga, a dialect of Algonquian Ojibway, na-pa-ni or nah-pah-nah meaning "a place of much flour."

Located on Lake Ontario between Toronto and Ottawa, the rural Canadian settlement of Napanee built one of the first gristmills in the area. Before the mill was erected, the community was known as Appanee or Apanee, after the Apanee River flowing nearby. An "n" was added for a more euphonious sound.

NATCHEZ (NAT-chez)
Village in southeast Martin County, est. 1844 (M-5)

The Martin County village honors Natchez, Mississippi, which was named after the Muskhogean-speaking tribe.

Surrounded by the Hoosier National Forest, Natchez, Indiana, may unknowingly, be descriptively named since the obscure word is believed to have roots from the Caddo Amer-Indian word, na'thcha, nachee, na'htchi or na'htcha'hi meaning "forest timberlands." Natchez may possibly mean "warriors of the high bluff."

NEBRASKA (ne-BRASK-ka)
Village in northeast Jennings County, est. 1856 (K-9)

The Nebraska Territory was created in 1854 and nearly three years later it was admitted to the Union as a State. Nebraska, Indiana, was probably named after the territory or in celebration of its impending Statehood.

The midwestern state is named for the former Nebraska River, now known as the Platte River. The Iowa, Oto and Omaha tribes knew it as ne-brath-kee, ne-prath-kae, ne-brath-kae, nebrathkane, niubthatkane or ne-bres-kuh meaning "flat, shallow and broad water." The French name, Platte, has the same definition. The low waters of the river make it unsuitable for boat transportation.

O-hee-yo, "beautiful river," Ohio River

OHIO (o-HI-o)
River forming the southern boundary of Indiana with Kentucky:
Kentucky counties: Boone, Gallatin, Carroll, Trimble, Oldham, Jefferson, Bullitt, Meade, Breckinridge, Hancock, Daviess, Henderson, Webster (L-P-1-11)
Indiana Counties: Dearborn, Ohio, Switzerland, Jefferson, Clark, Floyd, Harrison, Crawford, Perry, Spencer, Warrick, Vanderburgh, (L-P-1-1)
County in southeast Indiana, est. 1844 (L-10-11)
Townships in Crawford, est. 1818 (N-6), Bartholomew, est. 1821 (K-7), Spencer, est. 1818 (O-4) and Warrick, est. 1813 (O-4) counties

The French explorers used the Iroquois name, possibly of Seneca dialect, O-hee-yo meaning "the beautiful river" or "La Belle Riviere." The Ottawa called the river Oligh-in-sipu, the Wyandotte, Ohezuh, and the Shawnee, Spay Laweethippi; all three meaning the "grand or beautiful river.". The Miami Indian word was Oyo or Ohi and the Delaware, Ohiopukhanne, both meaning "beautiful river."

The Ohio River begins at Pittsburgh, Pennsylvania, at the junction of the Allegheny and Monongahela Rivers and flows 1,306 miles southwest to the confluence with the Mississippi River near Cario, Illinois.

ONTARIO (on-TEH-ri-o)
Village in north central Lagrange County, est. 1837 (A-9)

Ontario, Indiana, was named by early settlers after Lake Ontario, one of the five Great Lakes. Ontara, Onontario, or Oniatar is a Wyandotte Indian word of Iroquoian dialect meaning "beautiful great lake or waters" and was often called the "Lake of the Iroquois." Similar interpretations include "beautiful prospect of rocks, hills and water" and "village on the mountains overlooking the lake." The Wyandotte lived on the bay near Kingston, Ontario, and the St. Lawrence River. The word expresses the view from a portage trail at a summit overlooking the lake. Additional names for Lake Ontario include the Huron, Yontare, Iroquois, Oniatare, and Mohawk, Skanodario, all meaning "beautiful waters."

OPOSSUM CREEK (o-PAA-som kreek)
Stream in northwest Brown County

OPOSSUM RUN (o-PAA-som run)
Stream in southwest Warren County

Opossum (Didelphis marsupialis) is derived from a Algonquian speaking tribe in Virginia, possible Powhatan. The name a-pa-sum means "white animal" or "white beast."

The opossum is the only marsupial in North America. They are omnivorous, arboreal, and nocturnal mammals of streams as well as woodlands and farming areas. Some characteristics include having a prehensible tail, acting dead when threatened, and appearing much as their ancestors did a million years ago.

Opossum Creek is a north-to-south flowing stream, a tributary of Lake Lemon and Bean Blossom Creek in extreme northwest Brown County.

Opossum Run begins north of Johnsonville, Indiana, in Warren County and flows southeast to the Wabash River.

OREGON (OR-e-gon)
Townships in Clark County, est. 1801 (M-8) & Starke County, est. 1850 (C-5)

It appears the selection of the place name Oregon by the Indiana townships was influenced by events that took place in the Northwest Territory. According to a history of Clark County, "the Oregon Territory filled a larger space in the political history of the country." No doubt the "Oregon Fever" of the 1840's influenced the Starke County township to select the name.

Oregon is a French corruption of Ouragon or Oregones, an Algonquian word of Cree or Ojibway speech for a wooden dish or plate. The Columbia River was first known as the Oregon River, but was renamed in 1791. Supposedly the name was applied to the river in reference to its flat and quiet surface, "like the liquid in a birch bark dish."

Another source cites the name is personal, and of a Jesuit priest meaning "big eared man." The word was possibly transplanted from the Great Lakes to the Pacific Northwest by the French voyageurs.

OSCEOLA (o-see-OW-la)
Town in east central St. Joseph County, est. 1837 (B-7)

Several locales in many states, including Indiana, a-dopted the name of the most noted Seminole War Chief, Osceola (1803?-1838). According to historian, Wickham, Osceola was neither a Semi-nole or a Chief, but of mixed lineage, for his grandfather was a Scot and his primary family, Creek. His Creek name was Assiyahala, also spelled Asi-ya-hai or Yahola meaning, "black drink singer," in reference to the black tea made from the native yaupon holly leaves (Ilex vomitoria) the men drank at

Osceola or Assi-yahala,
"black drink singer,"
Seminole leader
painting from Thomas L. McKenney
& James Hall

ceremonies.

Osceola was born in Alabama along the Tallapoosa River (Creek, "pulverized rock"), a tributary of the Alabama River. In south Florida. Osceola led the Seminole during the Second Seminole War (1835-1842) against the American forces. He was captured and imprisoned at St. Moultrie, South Carolina, where he died in 1838 around the age of 35.

John A. Hendricks gave the Indiana community its name. Supposedly Mr. Hendricks was a friend of General Jessup, the soldier who captured Osceola. More than likely, he chose the name Osceola, who at the time was receiving a great amount of national press reports.

OSWEGO (os-WEE-go)
Village in north central Kosciusko County, est. 1837 (C-8)
Lake in Plain Township, Kosciusko County (C-8)

Oswego, Indiana, occupies the former location of the Potawatomi village of Chief Mes-qua-buck or Mus-qua-buck (1772-1836) his personal name meaning "copper colored" or "color at sunrise or sunset." The Indiana village is named for the New York community, county, and lake by settlers from upstate New York.

The Iroquoian word, osh-we-go, o-swe-go, osh-wa-kee, on-ti-ahan-toque or or swa-geh means, "the outpouring or flowing out," "small water flowing into what which is large" or "where the valley widens," in reference to where the Oswego River in New York empties into Lake Ontario. According to Beauchamp, the name belongs to the river, but was applied to the lake by the Onondaga and Oneida tribes.

The name is somewhat descriptive for the northern Indiana village where it is located near the outlet of Tippecanoe Lake, the headwaters of the Tippecanoe River. Oswego Lake is formed at the outlet of Tippecanoe Lake in the stream course of the Tippecanoe River, about a half mile north of the village.

OTISCO (o-TI-sko)
Village in north central Clark County, est. 1854 (M-8)

The transfer place name is derived from the Ostickney Indians, a subband of Onondaga, or "people of the hills," who were a major tribe of the Iroquois Confederacy of upstate New York. They lived in the area of Otisco Lake, one of the principal Finger Lakes, 14 miles southwest of Syracuse, New York.

Otisco means "water dried away." This Iroquoian language word refers to the receding waters of a once larger lake.

OTSEGO (ut-SEE-go)
Township in southeast Steuben County, est. 1837 (B-10)

Many of the early settlers of Otsego Township and Steuben County were originally from New York and New England and the place name appears to be a transfer.

The Iroquoian name, possibly Mohawk, Ote-sa-ga or Os-ten-ha means "rock site" or "place of the rock" refering to the large boulder at the outlet of Otsego Lake in upstate New York where it empties into Lake Ontario. The word Otsego is also reported to mean ot — "water," sego — "welcome" or "place where meetings are held." The northeastern lake is the scene of the **Deerslayer,** a classic by James Fenimore Cooper who also penned **The Last of the Mohicans.**

OWASCO (o-WAA-sko)
Village in southwest Carroll County, est. 1884 (F-5)

Owasco, Indiana, derives its commemorative name from 11-mile-long Owasco Lake, one of the upstate New York's Finger Lakes. The name O-was-co is Iroquoian and means "at the bridge," "lake of the floating bridge" or "floating bridge" and "outlet."

The Chicago, Indianapolis, Delphi, and Louisville Railroad Companies put the Hoosier town on the map. The railroad developers also may have descriptively named the village. Owasco, Indiana, is located on the south bank of Wildcat Creek where the railroad bridge crossed the stream.

PAPAKEECHIE LAKE (pa-pa-KEE-chee-lake)
Lake in northeast Kosciusko County (B-8)

Located southeast of Lake Wawasee, 178-acre Papakee-chie Lake is named in honor of Miami Chief Papakeechie or "Flat belly" (1765?-1839?), a brother of Chief Wawasee (see Wawasee, Waubee). Contrary to the anglized interpretation of his Miami name, Flatbelly was obese in his adult life.

After the War of 1812 and prior to 1821, Papakeechie's 36-section reserve covered most of Tippecanoe and Turkey Creek townships in northeast Kosciusko County, Washington, and

Indian Oven, historical marker at Indian Village, Indiana

Sparta townships in west central Noble County, The chief's brick home was located in Indian Village, Noble County, Indiana. In 1839, Papakeechie was reported to have left for Michigan, but other sources believe he died and was buried near Indian Village, Indiana.

PATOKA (pa-TOW-ka)
Stream of Orange, Dubois, Pike, & Gibson counties (M-N-2-6)
Lake reservoir in Orange & Dubois counties (M-N-5-6)
Town in Gibson County, est. 1789 (N-3)
Townships in Crawford, est. 1818 (N-6), Dubois, est. 1818 (N-5)
Gibson, est. 1813 (N-3), & Pike, est. 1817 counties (N-4)

The meaning of Patoka is obscure. Patoka may be a name for a chief, a description of the river, or Comanche slaves. The Kickapoo version says it is the name for a 19th century Wabash River chieftain of the Wolf Clan. To the Fox tribe, Pah-tah-ka-tah refers to the water depth or height on a wolf crossing the stream or "how deep." The Miami name Pah-to-kah may mean "snakes," their name for the Comanche, a High Plains tribe of Texas and Oklahoma. The Comanche that were captured were often used as slaves by other eastern tribes.

The lake reservoir, town, and townships were named after the 100-mile-long stream that heads in the hill country of southern

Orange and northern Crawford counties. The winding stream flows west to the Wabash River, picking up the South Fork Patoka River, about three miles north of the town of Oakland, Indiana.

PARISH GROVE (PEAR-rish grove)
Township in west central Benton County, est. 1840 (E-3)

Parish Grove was the summer home of a band of Prairie or Mascoten Potawatomi, the name derived from the chief, Parish, or Pierre Moran. Chief Parish was of French mixed blood, his father a French trader and his mother Kickapoo. Parish became a chieftain and fought in the Battle of Tippecanoe in 1811 with the Kickapoo. Later Parrish married a Potawatomi woman and became a Potawatomi chief, living near Black Rock, Indiana, near the Wabash River, home of his wife.

His name appears in writing on treaties as Peerish, Perish, Perig and Peannish. The name became anglized into Parish. Parish stuttered in his speech, hence his tribe called him Patach or Pa-ta-sha, signifying that in his speech, he became "fixed like frozen in mire, unable to proceed." Chief Parish was buried in his beloved grove of mixed hardwoods. The township bears his name.

Another historic grove of smaller size in Benton County was Turkey Foot Grove located between Fowler and Earl Park, Indiana. It was named after Turkey Foot or Pi-la-eugh-ka-ti, a Prairie Potawatomi subchief around the early 1800's.

Paw Paw Fruit, Paw Paw Creek, Miami County

PAW PAW CREEK (PAW-paw-kreek)
Streams in central Wabash & Miami counties (D-7-8) & Cass County (E-6)

Township in Wabash County, est. 1835 (D-7)

Paw Paw or papaw (Asimina triloba) is a small understory tree of stream bottoms and woodlands that bears an edible, custard-like fruit. The anglized name is probably a modification of the Spanish papaya (Carica papaya), a tropical American fruit tree. The word papaya is similar to the Otomac Indian word, papai or the word may be adapted from a Carib dialect. The Otomac are an extinct aboriginal people of southern Venezuela, South America.

Paw Paw Creek flows west to the Eel River from Wabash County to eastern Miami County between Roann and Chili, Indiana. Paw-Paw Creek is also a short stream that flows through France Park to join with the Wabash River. Paw Paw Township, Wabash County, is named after the stream.

PEORIA (pee-OW-ri-a)
Villages in east central Franklin County, est. 1850 (J-11) & southeast Miami County, est. 1849 (E-7)

Both of these small Hoosier communties were named for Peoria, Illinois, which was named in turn for a principal subtribe of the Illinois, Illini or Illiniweh Indian Confederacy. The origin and meaning of the name Peoria is questionable.

One possible but disputed source reports the anglized name is from the French word, Peouarea or Illinois word, Piwarea, meaning "one who carries a pack."

Another possible source reports the name may mean a wide or "fat" place on the Illinois River possibly Lake Peoria, the Illinois homeland of the Peoria, an Illini confederate. Another similar source reports that the Lake Peoria or Lake Pimitoui area is named for the abundance of game or "fat."

PERU (PER-ruu)
City, est. 1838, & township, est. 1834, in Miami County (E-7)

Peru, Indiana, was either named for Peru, New York, the home state of many early settlers or in sympathy for the South American country's struggle for independence from Spain in 1821.

The Spanish word, Peru is derived from Pelu of the Quechua language of the Incas. The word Pelu means "river." The Inca name for Peru is Tavantinsuyu meaning "four quarters of the world."

The former community known as Miamisport was adjacent to Peru and a rival for the county seat. Miamisport, now absorbed by Peru, was a trading post near the Wabash & Erie Canal and the Wabash River. The Miami name for the location was Ikkepissin-noong or "straight place" in reference to the two-mile straight stretch of Wabash River along the present-day city limits. The Delaware word was Conequonessing, "for a long time straight."

PIGEON RIVER (PI-geon)
Stream in Steuben & Lagrange counties (A-B-8-9-10)

The Potawatomi name for the northeast Indiana stream is Wahbememe or "white pigeon." The water body may be named for Wab-na-ne-me or "White Pigeon," a Potawatomi chief of light complexion, friendly to settlers. Supposedly, the chief saved an American settlement from an Indian uprising that today bears his name in southwest Michigan. The Potawatomi village of Mongo-quinong was situated along the north bank of the Pigeon River near Howe, Indiana. (see Mongo)

The lake-fed stream begins in south central Steuben County, flowing northwest to join with Turkey Creek, continuing through Lagrange County into Michigan to join the St. Joseph River.

PIPE CREEK (PIPE-kreek)
Stream in northwest Delaware County, north Madison County & extreme northeast Hamilton County (F-G-8-9)
Stream in northwest Grant County, south Miami County, & west central Cass County (E-7-8)
Stream in northeast Ripley County & south central Franklin County (J-K-10)
Pipe Creek-West Fork White River tributary:

Pipe Creek honors Delaware Chief Captain Pipe (1790's?-1818) or Hop-o-can, Hupoken, or Tahunquecoppi, "Tobacco Pipe." His Delaware name also appears as Ko-giesch-qua-no-hei or "Maker of Daylight." Pipe's village was near Orestes, Indiana, Madison County, where he is buried. Captain Pipe was a noted War Chief and active partisan of the British in the War of 1812.

Pipe Creek-Wabash River tributary:

The Miami knew this stream as Pwah-kah-nah, Piva-ka-na, or Pwa-ka-na meaning "pipe." The naming is unknown; however, it may relate to Indian peace tobacco pipes and council.

Big Pipe Creek joins with the Wabash River seven miles east of Logansport, Indiana, and Little Pipe Creek flows into the Wabash River two miles west of Peru, Indiana.

Pipe Creek-West Fork Whitewater River tributary:

The steam name is commemorative perhaps for an incident involving "peace" pipes. Located in Franklin and Ripley counties.

POKAGON STATE PARK (po-KAG-gon)
State park located in north central Steuben County, est. 1927 (A-10)

Colonel Richard Lieber, State Conservation Commissioner, suggested the name Pokagon for the state park in 1927 in honor of Leopold and his son Simon Pokagon, and the name was accepted.

According to fact and legend, Leopold Pokagon was a son of a Chippewa father and an Ottawa mother, born around 1775. His Chippewa name was Sakekwinik or Saqoquinick meaning "man of the river's mouth." He was captured by the Potawatomi and raised by Chief Topene-

Lepold Pokagon or "rib"
Potawatomi Chief
painting by Van Sandem

bee who gave him the name Pokagon meaning "rib," since he was wearing a rib in his hair from a warrior killed in battle upon capture. Pokagon rose quickly in the Potawatomi ranks and was made a chief. He died in the early 1800's when his son Simon was 11.

Simon Pokagon attended college at Notre Dame, Oberlin and Twinsburg, Ohio. He married a Potawatomi woman named Lonidaw, meaning, "spirit of the woods." His autobiography, **Ogimawke Mitigwaki** or **Queen of the Woods** reveals in a romantic nostalgic way the lifestyle of his family and the Potawatomi when his people were more attuned to nature. In 1893, Simon Pokagon and his family attended the Chicago World's Fair and transferred the deeds for their lands to the United States.

"Indian Funeral" Potawatomi, Kee-waw-nay Village, June 27, 1837
painting by George Winter

POTAWATOMI, POTTAWATTOMI, POTTAWATTOMIE
(po-ta-WAA-TA-mee)
Potawatomi Wildlife Park, park in southeast Marshall County (C-7)
Pottawattomi Park, village in northwest LaPorte County (A-5-6)
Potawatomi Point, village in central Cass County (E-6)
Potawatomi Zoo, at South Bend, Indiana (A-7)
Pottawattomie Lake, northeast LaPorte County (A-6)

The tribal name Potawatomi, Pottawattomi, Pottawattomie, or Putawame was used by the French explorers, but the Great Lakes tribe called themselves, Nesh-na-bek, "the true people." The Algonquian-names mean "the people of the place of fire," "fire maker nation" or "keepers of fire." The tribe is closely related to the northern Ottawa and Chippewa or Ojibwa.

Beginning in 1641, the Nesh-na-bek made several migrations south from the Straits of Mackinac, Michigan, to secure themselves from their enemies, the Sioux. They were the last of the historic tribes to enter Indiana. They were also among the last to be removed from Indiana to the west. Outstanding historic leaders of the northern Indiana Potawatomi include Metea, Menominee, Shipshewana, and Five Medals.

The Potawatomi made villages from the Kankakee River, east across northern Indiana. Their largest numbers were concentrated at the headwaters of the Tippecanoe River. The lake, villages, park, and zoo are named in honor of the tribe.

RACCOON (ra-KOON)
Village in north central Putnam County, est. 1880 (H-5)
State Recreation Area in east central Parke County (H-4)
Township in central Parke County, est. 1821 (H-5)
Streams in Boone, Montgomery, Owen, Parke, Putnam, & Ripley counties (F-K-2-10)

The name raccoon (Procyon lotor) is derived from Virginian Algonquian, possibly a Powhatan or Naraticong word, arahkun meaning "he scratches with the hand of trees" or "the scratcher." Additional spelling variants include: arakun, arocoun, arathkone, arratheune, racone, raugroughcum, rahaugcum and rarowcun.

The Miami named both Big and Little Raccoon Creeks, A-se-pa-na-si-pi-wi or Raccoon Creek, but knew them by different nick-names; che-kwi-ah or "a poor racoon" for Big Raccoon Creek and she-qui-hah or "a lean raccoon" for Little Raccoon Creek.

Big Raccoon Creek flows over 84.5 miles southwest and northwest to the Wabash River, at the Parke-Vermillion county line near Montezuma, Indiana. Little Raccoon Creek flows into Big Raccoon Creek near Jessups, Indiana, south central Parke County.

The village of Raccoon and Raccoon State Recreational Area on Cecil M. Harden Lake reservoir are named after the stream.

RED CLOUD (RED-cloud)
Village in central Knox County, est. 1875 (M-3)

The Knox County settlement most likely received its name from Red Cloud or Makhpiyaluta "scarlet cloud" (1822-1909), chief of the Oglala Teton Sioux at Pine Ridge Reservation, South Dakota.

He was born at the forks of the Platte River in Nebraska and died at the Pine Ridge Reservation. Red Cloud's Indian name was also spelled Mahpiyaluta and Makhipia-sha. Although lesser known, Red Cloud ranked as equally in leadership stature as Tatanka Iyotake or "Sitting Bull" (1834?-1890) and Tashunca-Uitco or "Crazy Horse" (1849?-1877).

The origins of Red Cloud's Anglo name is disputed, but is said by McGillycuddy to refer to the way in which his scarlet-blanketed warriors covered the hillsides, "like a scarlet cloud."

ROANOKE, ROANOKE STATION (ROW-noke,
ROW-noke-station)
Town & settlement in northeast Huntington County, est. 1846
(D-9)

According to an unsigned letter by a local historian, Roanoke received its name via Roanoke, Virginia:

> "Colonel Samuel G. Jones of Ft. Wayne, knowing the excellent quality of the lands for timber and agriculture of the surrounding country, also considered the location for a town a good one. He secured 800 acres of land for "Roanoke Farms" from his admiration of John Randolph of Roanoke, Virginia. When appointed the first postmaster at the Indiana village, the name given the office was selected. The village took the name from the farm and the postoffice."

It is also believed the town of Roanoke was named after a saw mill company called Roanoke Mills that located here in 1845.

The Algonquian name is Secotan for wampum or "shell bead money." Several types of shells were exchanged including snails, clams, oysters and mussels. The Secotan Indians gave the name Roanoke to an offshore North Carolina island where the shells could be found. Roanoke is the Virginia and Carolina-Algonquian equivalent of New England wampum, polished shell beads strung in strands, belts or sashes.

Variant spellings of Roanoke include roenoke, rawrenock, rawranoke, roenoak, ronoak and roanoak.

RUSSIAVILLE (RUU-sha-vil)
Village in southwest Howard County, est. 1845 (H-4)

Russiaville is a corruption of the namesake Richardville, the anglized name of Peshewa, Pin-je-wah, Pe-che-wa, or Pee-jee-wah meaning "the wild cat" (1761-1841). Richardville or Pin-je-wah was born at the main Miami village of Kekionga, now Ft. Wayne, the son of a French trader, Joseph Drouet de Richardville and Miami mother, Taucumwah or Tah-kum-wah, sister of Little Turtle.

Pin-je-wah participated in the defeat of American General Harmar, October 1790. Upon the death of Little Turtle, Pin-je-wah became the principal Miami Chief or Sachem, the last head Chief of the Miamis. Pin-je-wah married Pemesequah and reared four sons, one of which was Kokomo. After five American-Indian treaties between 1818-1840, Richardville had obtained 44 sections of Wabash Valley lands. The Big Miami Reserve encompassed Howard County, the largest historical Indian reserve in Indiana. Richardville became wealthy dealing in furs at Kekionga.

Nearly 80 years old, Pin-je-wah or Jean John Baptiste Richardville died at his home on the St. Marys River in Ft. Wayne, August, 1841. Howard County was first known as Richardville County and Wildcat Creek is named in his honor. (see Wildcat)

SALAMONIA, SALAMONIE (sal-la-MOW-nee)
Town in southeast Jay County, est. 1839 (F-11)
Township in Huntington County, est. 1834 (E-8)
Lake reservoir in Huntington & Wabash counties, est. 1966 (E-8)
Stream of Jay, Blackford, Wells, Huntington & Wabash counties (D-F-8-10)
State Forest near Lagro, Indiana, Wabash County (D-8)

The bloodroot (Sanguinaria canadensis) is the name source of the Salamonie River. The Miami know the lovely spring wild-flower as o-sah-mo-nee, oh-za-la-mo-ni or o-sah-da-mo-nee meaning "yellow paint." The stream was probably named for the abundance of the herbaceous plant growing along the banks, which the Miami gathered to produce the yellow dye and for medicine. Chief O-sah-la-mo-nee or Le Gros lived at the mouth of the Salamonie River, where the stream joins with the Wabash River at present day Lagro, Indiana. (see Lagro)

Salamonia, the Latinized feminine form of Salamonie, is a town located in Jay County near the headwaters. The township, lake reservoir, and state forest are named after the stream. Spelling variants include Sallimony, Salimony and Salamoniah.

SALUDA (sa-LUU-da)
Creek, village, est. 1828, & township, est. 1811, southwest Jefferson County (M-9)

Saluda is probably Cherokee and was first named for a west central South Carolina river that flows southeast to unite with the Broad River, to later form the Congaree River. Saluda or selutah means "a river of corn" or "corn river," selu meaning "corn" and tah,"river." The Saluda were also a small tribe formerly living near the Saluda River in the southeast, but were removed to Penn-sylvania in the early 18th century. The name may be possibly con-nected with the Shawnee.

The creek was named first and in turn was the source of the place name for the township and village.

SANDUSKY (SAN-dusk-kee)
Village in north central Decatur County, est. 1882 (J-9)

Sandusky, Indiana, is a transfer name from the Buckeye State within Ohio; Sandusky is a city, county, river and bay on Lake Erie. Spelled in various ways, Sandusky's roots are possibly from the Wyandotte word, otsaandost meaning "cool, cold pure water," perhaps referring to a spring at the original Indian village.

Two Wyandotte villages were formerly in the Sandusky, Ohio, area, one settled in 1751 by a party of Hurons, who later became known as Wyandottes.

SARATOGA (se-ra-TOW-ga)
Town in northeast Randolph County, est. 1875 (F-10)

More than likely, Saratoga, Indiana, is a transfer name from upstate New York via early settlers from the region. Most authorities believe Saratoga is derived from the Mohawk or Iroquois word, ochsechrage, oschseratongue, or se-rach-ta-que meaning "sparkling place," "springs from a hillside," "hillside country of the great river," "place of swift water," or "the place where ashes float" or "beaver place."

According to Macauley, 19th century American historian, it is a name of a Mohawk band formerly occupying the west bank of the Hudson River near Saratoga, New York.

SHAKAMAK (SHACK-a-mack)
Lake & state park in northwest Greene County (K-3-4)

Shakamak or Schack-a-mek is the Delaware word for the Eel River of southwestern Indiana, a major tributary of the west fork White River. Schack-a-mek refers to the snake-like eels (Anguilla rostrata) that inhabit the water and means "slippery long fish." Shakamak State Park and Lake are named for the river. (see Eel River, north & south)

SHANKITUNK CREEK, SHANKATANK CREEK
(SHANG-ki-tunk-kreek, SHANG-KA-tank-kreek)
Stream in lower Henry County and northeast Rush County (H-9)

The Delaware knew the creek as Choak-hit-tuck or "big tree creek" or "shady place." The north-to-south stream joins with the Big Flat Rock River, northeast of Rushville, Indiana. The present-day name is probably a corruption of the Delaware name for the stream.

SHAWNEE (SHAW-nee)
Streams in Tippecanoe & Fountain counties (F-4-5)
Township in Fountain County, est. 1846 (F-4)
Stream of northeast Rush & northwest Fayette counties (H-9)

Shawnee means "southerners" or "people of the south wind" and may be derived from the Algonquian word, Shaw-unogi or Shawandasse. The Miami called them Sha-ha-han-way or Shah-wahn-wah and the Delaware, Shawanan. Prior to being forced north by the Cherokee, Creek, and Choctaw, the Shawnee lived in present-day Georgia, north Florida and the Carolinas. Originally it is believed the Delaware may have been forced south from the Susquehanna River (corruption of Delaware, Suckahanni, "pure waters") area of Pennsylvania by the Iroquois Confederacy.

The Shawnee entered Indiana from the southeast around 1684-1790, after being invited by the Miami. Their nation was Algonquian-speaking and consisted of four main tribes: Piqua, Mequachabe, Kiskapocke and Chillicothe. Some outstanding leaders of the Shawnee nation include Tecumseh, his brother Tenskwatawa, better known as "The Prophet," Blue Jacket, Cornstalk, Black Hoof, White Fish and Silver Heels.

Big Shawnee Creek's headwaters are in southwest Tippecanoe County, flowing westwards through northern Fountain County in an area known as Shawnee Prairie, to the Wabash River. Little Shawnee Creek joins with Big Shawnee Creek near Rob Roy, Indiana. Shawnee Chief Chippay or Chipaille had a village at the mouth of the stream. Shawnee Creek in northeast Rush County is a tributary of the Big Flat Rock River.

SHIPSHEWANA (SHIP-shee-waa-na)
Lake & creek in northwest Lagrange County (A-8)
Town in northwest Lagrange County, est. 1888 (A-8)

The town, lake, and stream are named in honor of Potawatomi Chief Shipshewana (1800's?-1841) oftentimes spelled Shup-she-wah-no or Cup-ci-wa-no, whose band lived at Shipshewana Lake. The personal name may have come to him in a boyhood dream about a cougar (Felis concolor) or possibly derived from a woman who had a vision in his village at the time of his birth. The name is said to mean "vision of a lion."

Shipshewana Memorial, "vision of a lion," Shipshewana Lake

Evidence of the chief and his band may be found inscribed on the lakeside monument dedicated to Chief Shipshewana May 30, 1931. The plaque reads, "The Chief was removed from this reservation September 4, 1838 and was escorted to Kansas by a company of soldiers. He returned in 1839 and died in 1841."

Additional spelling variants of his name include Ship-Shewanne, Ship-She-Wahn-O, Shipshee Wano, Shep-She-Wa-No, Shup-She-Wa-No, Shuv-A-Aw-No, Shipe-Ghe-Wash-No, Shep-Shau-Wah-No, Chup-Si-Wah-No, Shav-C-Aw-No, and Shep-She.

SITKA (SIT-ka)
Village in northeast White County, est. 1880 (E-5)

In 1880, M. Allison Hughes was required to have a place name for the establishment of a post office for the White County settlement. Mr. Hughes chose Sitka, the capitol of the Alaska Territory and fomer capitol of Russian-America (1804-1867).

Sitka is believed to be a Tlingit word from Shitka possibly meaning "by the sea." Shitka is a native place name for Sitka, Alaska, and the entire Baronof Island, situated in the Alexander Archipelago on the Pacific Ocean.

SQUIRREL CREEK (SKWOR-ril-kreek)
Creek in northeast Miami & extreme northwest Wabash counties (D-7-8)

Squirrel Creek is approximately 11.2 miles long, heading in Miami County, Indiana, and flowing southeast to its confluence at the Eel River in Wabash County, about one-quarter mile east of the Miami-Wabash County line at Stockdale, Indiana.

Squirrel Creek is a literal translation of Niconga, Niconza, or Ni-con-ga, a Potawatomi chief who lived at the stream's confluence with the Eel River. Ne-quah means "squirrel" in Miami and he was also known as "Captain Squirrel." The chief was also believed to have had villages on Pipe Creek in south Miami County and Thorntown, Boone County.

STRAWTOWN (STRAW-town)
Village in northeast Hamilton County, est. 1834 (G-7)

Supposedly Strawtown was a historic Delaware village located one and one-half miles upriver from the present-day village along the south bank of the West Fork White River. The village of

Strawtown was named for Chief Straw or Strawbridge. Moravian missionaries who lived among the White River Delaware, account for an Indian village. A monument was erected to the memory of the chief of Strawtown, Indiana, marking the location where he is supposedly buried.

However, according to other researchers, there is no conclusive evidence to show Strawtown was a historic Delaware village, or that there actually was a Chief Straw or Strawbridge. Chamberlain, regional historian, writes that the name may simply have been derived from a residence thatched with straw.

SUGAR CREEK (SHUU-gar-kreek)
Stream in Clinton, Boone, Montgomery & Parke counties (F-G-H-3-4-5-6)
Townships in Clinton, est. 1830 (F-6), Boone, est. 1830 (G-6), Montgomery, est. 1823 (G-5) & Parke counties, est. 1821 (H-4)

The Miami name for this scenic west central Indiana stream is Ke-an-kik-se-pe, Sa-na-min-dji-sipi-wi or Sa-na-nun-dji-sipi-wi, or "sugar tree creek," named after the sugar maple (Acersaccharum). Maple sugaring was a source of sweetness for the Native Americans of the northeastern United States, who tapped the trees during late winter, along stream bank encampments and north facing upland slopes of ravines and hillsides. The 100-mile-long stream flows through Shades and Turkey Run state parks before joining the Wabash River, north of Montezuma, Indiana.

There are several streams known as Sugar Creek in Indiana and probably all are named in honor of the sweet maple tree. Sugar Creek of Henry, Hancock, Shelby, Franklin, and Bartholomew counties was formerly called Achsinnaminschi by the Delaware and Huron meaning "the name say."

TECUMSEH (ta-KUM-saa)
Village in north central Vigo County, est. 1840 (J-3)

Tecumseh, Indiana was established by Dr. John Durkee near the confluence of Otter Creek and the Wabash River, just upstream from Terre Haute, Indiana. Dr. Durkee ran a ferry service, and at first, the settlement was known as Durkee's Ferry until 1840 when the named changed in honor of the Shawnee Chief Tecumtha, Tecum-tha, Ti-kam-thi, or Tecumseh (1768-1813), who is said to have encamped on the village site. Tecumseh was born along the Mad River near Old Piqua, Ohio, near present-day Springfield, Ohio,

Tecumseh and Harrison
painting by Chapin

to his Shawnee father, Puckeshinwa and Creek mother, Methoas-
tashe. It is said on the night of Tecumseh's birth, a meteor traversed
across the sky, an omen of great destiny. The brilliant object
influenced his mother who named her fifth child, Tecumthe,
Tecumtha, "Shooting Star," "meteor crossing the sky," or "one who
passes across intervening space, from one point to another." The
Algonquian name is also said to mean "crouching panther."

Many of Tecumseh's family were killed in American-Shawnee
conflicts. Together with his brother, Lawlewasikaw or Lalawe-
thika, "the loud voice," later known as Elkswatawa and later
Tenskwatawa, "an open door to the Great Spirit Mandamon," they
became ardent opponents of the American advancement into their
lands and great orators for a pan-American Indian movement.
Dedicating their lives to the Indian cause, the brothers undertook
the formation of a confederacy of all tribes to hold the Euro-
American advancement at the Greenville Treaty Line.

Their dreams were vanished at the November 11, 1811, Battle of
Tippecanoe. Tecumseh was later killed at the Battle of Thames,
Ontario, Canada, during the War of 1812 at age 45 by American forces. His brother better known as Tenskwatawa, "The Prophet" died
of old age at an Oklahoma reservation years later.

THORNTOWN (THORN-town)
Town in northwest Boone County, est. 1831 (G-5)

An Indian village, possibly Miami, existed as early as 1719, on the present-town site of Thorntown, Indiana. The village was called Keewaskee, Ka-wi-a-ki-un-gi or Kah-we-ash-ki-oon-gi meaning "place of thorns," perhaps in reference to an abundance of hawthorn trees. (Crataegus sp.) and honey locust (Gleditsia triacanthos) that grew on thinner soils. Between 1818 and 1828, the site was one of the principal Indian reservations west of Pittsburgh, Pennsylvania, primarily occupied by the Eel River Miami. The site was also known as Ten-Mile Reservation.

TIOSA (tie-OW-saa)
Village in northeast Fulton County, est. 1869 (C-7)

Potawatomi Chief Tiosa or Toisa's village of about 50 people was situated on the west bank of the Tippecanoe River near Talma, Indiana, during the early 19th century. The present-day village of Tiosa is located a few miles west of the river where the former Norfolk and Western railroad operated.

Tiosa means, "beaver" or "friend" in Potawatomi. The chief went west in 1837 in a removal conducted by George Proffitt, U.S. military officer.

TIPPECANOE (ti-pee-ka-NUU)
Stream of Kosciusco, Marshall, Fulton, Pulaski, White, Carroll & Tippecanoe counties (C-D-E-5-6-7)
Lake of northeast Kosciusko County (C-8)
Towns in south Marshall County, est. 1850 & 1882 (C-7)
Townships in Kosciusko, est. 1837 (C-8), Marshall, est. 1836, (C-6), Pulaski, est. 1840 (D-5), Carroll County, est. 1828, (E-6) & Tippecanoe, est. 1826 counties (F-5)
County in northwest Indiana, est. 1826 (F-5)
State Park in east central Pulaski County (C-D-5-6)
National Historic Landmark, State Memorial & county park in northeast Tippecanoe County (F-5)

The place name Tippecanoe became a national household word when General William "Tippecanoe" Henry Harrison and his "Yellow Jackets" destroyed Prophetstown, an Indian warrior village, after the Battle of Tippecanoe in 1811. The river's name is derived from a pre-Prophetstown village of Miami and Shawnee known as Kithtippecanunk, Kithtippeconmunk, or Kath-tip-e-ca-nunk, located downstream from the Tippecanoe-Wabash confluence that had been destroyed earlier in 1791 by American forces. The Indian name translates to mean "place of buffalo fish" (Ictiobus cyprinellus). It may also mean "at the clearing" or "long water space" from kithlippi.

The Miami called the Tippecanoe River, Ke-tap-kwon or Ke-tup-kwan. Prophetstown was the American name for the village of the Shawnee prophet or shaman, Tenskwatawa, "one who keeps open door to the Great Mystery," brother of Tecumseh. Prophetstown was a two mile long, bluff-top military town along the Wabash River, located between the confluence of the Tippecanoe River and Wildcat Creek.

The headwaters of the Tippecanoe River, "the river of lakes," begins at Tippecanoe Lake, the deepest lake in Indiana, located in east central Kosciusko County. The stream flows south and west 220 miles to the confluence with the Wabash River, passing through and near Old Tipp Town, Tippecanoe, Indiana, Tippecanoe State Park, and various townships by the name of Tippecanoe. Tippecanoe Battlefield Memorial Park is located at Battleground, Indiana. Palestine, Indiana, was known at first as Tipicanunk, a form of Tippecanoe from 1830-1839.

TOPEKA (ta-PEE-ka)
Town in southwest Lagrange County, est. 1843 (B-8)

Most authorities believe the name Topeka means "a good place to dig wild potatoes or any edible root." Topeka is derived from Siouan Kansa, Oto or Omaha, To-pe-o-ka, To-pe-o-kae, or To-pyo-kae, a word used by the Plains Indians to designate food roots, particularly Jerusalem artichoke (Helianthus tuberosa).

Topeka, Indiana, was originally known as Haw Patch until the name changed in 1893 in honor of the Kansas capital.

TOTO (TOW-tow)
Village in west central Starke County, est. 1855 (C-5)

Toto may possibly be an Indian word of unclear meaning and uncertain origin, but possibly Algonquian for "bullfrog." Toto may also have been derived from totowa or totua possibly meaning "to begin from," "to dive and surface," or "land bridge."

TRAIL CREEK (TRAIL-kreek)
Stream, town, est. 1923 & township, est. 1832 in northwest

LaPorte County (A-B-5)

A Potawatomi foot trail followed the south bank of Trail Creek, enroute from Chicago, Illinois, to Niles, Michigan, once part of the Potawatomi-Sauk Trail network between Rock Island, Illinois, and Detroit, Michigan. The native name for the stream is Me-eh-we-se-bi-weh or Mi-e-we-si-bi-we literally translating to mean "trail creek." Having a similar meaning, the French called the stream Riviere du Chemin or "River of the Pathway."

Trail Creek is formed from the confluence of the East Branch Trail Creek and the West Branch Trail Creek, just southeast of the town Trail Creek, in LaPorte County. Trail Creek flows north and west seven miles through Michigan City, Indiana, to Lake Michigan. The town and township are named after the stream.

Creek Ridge, a LaPorte County Park, features nature trails along the west branch of the stream in Cool Springs Township, south of Michigan City.

VERMILLION (vur-MIL-li-on)
Streams, township, est. 1824 & County, est. 1824 in west Central Indiana (H-3)

O-san-amon was the Piankeshaw or Kickapoo name given to the French-named Vermillion River that flows east and south from the Illinois prairie to join with the Wabash River north of Newport, Indiana. An important Piankeshaw town was located at the mouth of the Big Vermillion River along the north bank just below Cayuga, Indiana. Battles were fought for its strategic position.

Osanamon means "yellow red" or "vermillion paint," a bright red-orange ocher consisting of mercuric sulfide. The fine red and yellow clay or keel was found along the banks and used for paint for skins, bows, arrows, dugouts, and dress. The Miami name for the Piankeshaw town was Alamoni, their name for vermillion or "red paint." The French name of the river was Vermilion Jaune or "red yellow."

The county and township are named after the Vermillion River. The Little Vermillion River also heads in Illinois and joins the Wabash River near Newport and Eugene, Indiana.

WABASH (WAW-bash)
River in Indiana counties of Adams, Wells, Huntington, Wabash, Miami, Cass, Carroll, Tippecanoe, Warren, Fountain, Vermillion, Parke, Vigo, Sullivan, Knox, Gibson, & Posey (D-P-3-10)

River in Illinois counties of Clark, Crawford, Lawrence, Wabash, Edward, White, Gallatin (J-P-1-4)
College, est. 1832 in Crawfordsville, Indiana (G-5)
County, est. 1835 in north central Indiana (D-E-7-8)
City, est. 1827 (E-8) city & county seat of Wabash County, est. 1827 (E-8) Townships in Jay, est 1836 (E-10), Adams, est. 1836 (E-10), Tippecanoe, est. 1826 (F-5), Fountain, est. 1826 (G-4), Parke, est. 1821 (H-4), & Gibson counties, est. 1813 (N-3)
Little (Wabash) River: Allen & Huntington counties (C-D-8-9-10)
State Park in east central Wells County (E-10)

"Sunrise from Hanging Rock," Wabash River near Largo, Indiana

The Wabash River is Indiana's State River and has long been immortalized in poetry, legend, and song. The nearly 500-mile-long stream drains most of Indiana's landscape flowing northwest, west, and south to the Ohio River. Many Indian-named tributaries flow into the "Father of Indiana Waters" including the Salamonie, Mississinewa, Tippecanoe, Vermillion, and others.

Wabash is a shortened anglized name derived from the Miami, Wah-bah-shik-ki, Wah-bah-shay-ke, Wah-sah-shay-ke, Wa-ba-ci-ki, Wa-pa-ci-ki, or Waubache meaning "white or pure bright water," "water flowing over white stones," "white path," or "white like the inside of a mussel shell." Waub-o-shee is also said to be "white clouds borne by the wind." The name refers to the white Niagara limestone bed in the upper course of the river, roughly from Ft. Recovery, Ohio, to Logansport, Indiana.

Ouabache is the French Jesuit spelling of the Miami pronunciation and the early voyageurs translated the Indian name to mean "singing river." Ouabache State Park is located along the Wabash River east of Bluffton, Indiana.

The Little River, often called the Little Wabash River, was known by the Miami as Paw-we-kom-se-pe or "no current river," but it is a major tributary fork of the upper Wabash River at the highway junction of U.S. 24 and S.R. 9 west of Huntington, Indiana. The location is the historic "Forks of the Wabash."

WACO (WAY-ko)
Village in southwest Daviess County, est. 1891 (M-4)

Waco, Indiana, was named for the southeast Texas city, located between Dallas, Houston, and Austin. Many reliable sources believe the anglized name form is from the Caddoan (or "Real Chiefs") language family and is the name of a Wichita band known as Weko meaning "heron." Waco has also been derived from Seminole, wako or "little blue heron" (The Potawatomi word for big blue heron is wawaka). The name may also be from Wehico, a corruption of the Mexican word. In addition, Waco may be from a Wichita word meaning "big arbor" or tawakoni, "river bend among red sand hills."

The Indiana settlement is located within the Glendale State Fish & Wildlife Area in southwestern Indiana and is nearly non-existent.

WADENA (wa-DEE-na)
Village in north central Benton County, est. 1884 (E-4)

Wadena was given its name by John Swan, who had been traveling through the state of Minnesota and was so impressed with the town of Wadena, Wadena County, he chose the name for the Benton County, Indiana, community.

Wadena is belived to be an altered version of the old Ojibway name waud-ekaw meaning "little round hill." The place name may be applied descriptively at the prairie village of Wadena, Indiana, since it was established near

"little round hill" near Wadena

800 foot Mt. Nebo, one of the highest points and best vistas in Benton County.

WAKARUSA (wa-ka-RUU-sa)
Town in southwest Elkhart County, est. 1852 (B-7)

The place name was suggested by a Mr. Woolverton, one of the early town settlers, in honor of Wakarusa, Kansas, where he had lived earlier. The Kansas community is named after Wakarusa Creek whose tributary waters feed the Kansas River, east of Lawrence, Kansas.

Sources report the Shawnee name with its numerous spelling variants means "the river bank of the wild milkweeds" or possibly "hip deep (in mud)." Mr. Woolerton probably considered the latter interpretation because of the boggy soil at the town site.

WANATAH, SOUTH WANATAH (WAA-na-taa, south)
Towns in southwest LaPorte County, est. 1857 (B-5)

Potawatomi Chief Wanatah lived on or near the location of the present-day northwest Indiana communities. Wanatah or Wa-na-tah means "he who charges his enemies."

Local reports say the word is Indian for "knee deep in mud" referring to Hawk Creek or Slocum Ditch and the wet prairies that would mire wagons in the early years of settlement. The Potawatomi village of Tasinong or Tesinong was located south and west of Wanatah near the Kankakee River, and is said to mean "the flat country."

WAWASEE, WAUBEE (wa-WAA-SEE, WAW-bee)
Village, est. 1893 & lake in northeast Kosciusco County (B-8)
Waubee Lake in north central Kosciusco County (B-8)

Wah-we-as-see, Wah-wa-as-pee, Wau-waa-ussee, Waw-wa-esse, or Wa-wi-as-pi meaning "full moon" or the "round one" (1760's?-1839?) was a minor Miami Chief and purported brother of Papakeechie or "Flat Belly." Wah-we-as-see's village was situated in Van Buren Township near the southeast edge of present-day Waubee or Wabee Lake, two and one-half miles from Milford, Indiana. His nickname, Waubee or Wabee accounts for the name of the nearby smaller lake.

Prior to being named Lake Wawasee, the largest natural lake in Indiana was known as Nine Mile Lake or Big Turkey Lake. Eli Lilly is reported to have changed the name to Lake Wawasee. The village of Wawasee, formerly called Cedar Beach, is located on the north shore of the 2,618 acre lake.

Supposedly Chief Wah-we-as-see and his brother Pap-pakeechie returned from the western reservation and finally disappeared into Michigan around 1839 or died shortly thereafter in the lake area. (see Papakeechie)

WAWAKA (wa-WAA-ka)
Village in north central Noble County, est. 1857 (B-8)

Wawaka is a Potawatomi word meaning "big (blue) heron" (Ardea herodias). Chief Onaska or Five Medal's village was located downstream along the upper Elkhart River in St. Joseph County. The Potawatomi War Chief received his Anglo name from the medals he received from U.S. Presidents Washington and Jefferson after ceasing hostilities in 1795. Five Medals' village was destroyed in 1812 and again in 1813.

Wawpecong or "hickory grove"

WAWPECONG (WAA-pi-kong)
Village in south central Miami County, est. 1849 (E-7)

The place name Wawpecong is derived from the Miami word wa-pi-pa-ka-na meaning, "place of the shell bark hickories" (Carya ovata and C. lacinosa). Wawpecong, spelled historically on maps as Wapecong and Waupecong, is situated at the fertile headwaters of Deer Creek or Passeanong, "place of the fawn." The edible nuts and useful hardwood was of value to the Indians.

The place name is also said to have been obtained from an old Delaware village, Wah-pe-hon, meaning "white bone," located south of the present village.

WEA (WEE-a)
Streams, township & settlements in south central Tippecanoe County (F-4-5)

The Wea were a Miami subtribe or band who settled along the Big and Little Wea creeks, tributaries of the Wabash River, downstream from Lafayette, Indiana.

The name Wea is of uncertain derivation and meaning. Wea is an abbreviated form of Wah-we-ah-tun-ong, Wi-ah-ton-oon-gi, Wawiagtinang, Warviaqtenang, We-au-te-non, and Wah-wee-ah-anon, possibly meaning "the current goes" or "bend of stream." The Algonquian name Wawaqtenang was applied to the present-day Detroit River where the Wea once lived at the "place of the curved or round channel, where the eddy people lived." The French name for the tribe was Ouia and their village and trading post was called Ouiatenon, Ouiatenons, Ougatenons or Wyatenons. Additonal spelling variations of Wea include Onyatanous, Wyohtomas, and Wyaw.

The Wea were first known in the vicinity of Starved Rock, Chicago, Illinois, the St. Joseph River of Lake Michigan, and the headwaters of the Wabash River. The tribe were first recorded living in Tippecanoe County as early as 1695. One tradition says Wayoakeentonwau, a tribal leader, established a village on Wea Creek. It is reported the leader's name meant "whirlpool," and the Wea Prairie is named for him. (see Miami)

WEASEL CREEK, WEASAW CREEK
(WEE-zol-kreek, WEE-saw-kreek)
Stream in northwest Miami County (D-7)

Weasel Creek is the English rendition for the Miami wi-saw, we-saw, or weesaw meaning "animal gall bladder." The 10-mile-long stream usually appears on local maps as Wesaw or Weasau Creek. Little Weasel or Weasaw Creek is a tributary of the larger stream.

Chief Wi-saw, also known as Loueson, was granted a reserve near the mouth of the stream at the confluence with the Eel River near Denver, Indiana, in 1828. The creek flowed through his one-section reserve.

WELLS COUNTY (WELLS-county)
County in northeast Indiana, est. 1837 (E-9)

Apekonit is the Miami name of Captain William H. Wells, for

The Death of Captain William Wells by Winamac
painting by Wil Vawter

whom Wells County, Indiana, is named in honor. His Miami personal name signifies "wild carrot" in regard to his red hair; however, other sources say Apekonit means "Indian potato," "wild bean," or "ground nut."

William H. Wells was born of Euro-American parents at Jacob's Creek, Pennsylvania, in 1770. Wells was kidnapped by the Miami in Kentucky at the age of 11. Chief Little Turtle adopted Wells and later he married Little Turtle's daughter Manwangopath or "Sweet Breeze." Wells served as a military aide to Tecumseh during the defeats of Generals Harmar and St. Clair in Ohio. As a warrior, Apekonit was known as "Black Snake."

Later William Wells moved back to the American cause, parting as friends of the Miami. Wells joined General Wayne and fought on the American side at the Battle of Fallen Timbers 1794. Captain Wells died in an American-Indian conflict while leading an army garrison from Ft. Dearborn at Lake Michigan to Ft. Wayne, Indiana, August 15, 1812.

WHITE CLOUD (WHITE-cloud)
Village in west central Harrison County, est. 1879 (N-7)

White Cloud, Indiana, was founded by William Rothrock in 1880 and was named by his wife Mary Ann McCullum, supposedly, for the Indian medicine man, prophet, and Chief Wa-bo-kie-shiek or White Cloud (1794-1841), who was of mixed Winnebago and Sauk blood.

During the Sauk War of 1832 White Cloud served as an advisor to the Sauk War Chief Black Hawk (see Black Hawk) and was said to be the influence behind the uprising. Prophetstown, his village on the Rock River in northwest Illinois, was destroyed by Federal troops May, 1832.

The place name may also be descriptive.

WHITE EYE TRAIL (WHITE-eye-trail)
Designates thirty-five mile section of S.R. 62, from Madison, Indiana northeast to Dillsboro, Indiana (L-9-10)

This beautiful stretch of southern Indiana highway follows the former route of Chief White Eye and his people. The personal Indian name of Chief White Eye is unknown, and so are other details such as what tribe was he a member of since there are four cited in the literature: Shawnee, Potawatomi, Wyandotte and Delaware. The most reliable source cites that White Eye was Delaware; however, two historical markers in Jefferson County specify Wyandotte. There was a Delaware Captain White Eyes that lived in the Muskingum ("moose-eye") River Valley of eastern Ohio, whose Delaware name was Koguethagechton and who died of smallpox in 1778, the same approximate year that the Indiana White Eye was born.

Historians tells us that White Eye did sign a treaty with the United States in 1800 by which his tribe ceded lands in the Jefferson County area. Later, he was viewed as a renegade by the pioneers. After the nearby Pigeon Roost Massacre in 1812, White Eye was killed by two settlers in what is now-known as White Eye Hollow, a tributary of Indian-Kentuck Creek.

A historical memorial marker at the road junction of S.R. 62 and C.R. 250 reads:

> "Memorial and burial site of a Wyandotte Chief killed by white settlers after the Pigeon Roost massacre, 1812, age 30 years (?). Grave was first hidden up White Eye Hollow and relocated in 1965. White Eye was over 6' tall, wore long black hair with buzzard quills, breech cloth, confederate leggings, and blanket over his shoulder. He bred horses for early Jefferson County settlers with his stallion, Black Eagle."

A second monument is located at Neavills Grove near Volga, Indiana, in west Jefferson County.

WHITE RIVER, EAST & WEST FORKS
(WHITE-river, east and west forks)
Stream of central & southern Indiana (G-N-1-11)
White River: Pike, Gibson & Knox counties (M-N-2-3-4)
East Fork of White River: Bartholomew, Jackson, Washington, Lawrence, Martin, Dubois, Pike and Daviess counties (K-L-M-4-8)
West Fork of White River: Randolph, Delaware, Madison, Hamilton, Marion, Johnson, Morgan, Monroe, Owen, Greene, Daviess, & Knox counties (G-M-4-11).
Townships in Hamilton County, est. 1823, Johnson County, est. 1823 (J-6) & Gibson County, est. 1813 (N-3)

After the Wabash River, the White River is the longest statewide stream and could be accepted as the "State" river by many Hoosiers. The forks of the White River join near Petersburg, Indiana, flowing 50 westward miles more to the confluence with the Wabash River in Gibson County.

The West Fork was known by the Miami as Wahpikahmeki, or Wapeksippei, and Wapihanne, Wapihani, or Wapi-hanne by the Delaware, both meaning "white waters." The sun-exposed gravel and sand bars were said to be a white sheen of luster. The Delaware are known to have had 14 villages along the West Fork and several villages along the East Fork.

The East Fork was also known as the Driftwood Fork, draining much of southeast Indiana. The East Fork is supposedly a translation of the Miami, on-gwah-soh-kah literally meaning "driftwood." (see Driftwood)

WHITEWATER RIVER, EAST & WEST FORKS
(WHITE-water-river, east and west forks)
Stream of Randolph, Wayne, Union, Franklin, & Dearborn counties (G-K-9-10)
Town in northeast Wayne County, est. 1828 (G-11)
Township in Franklin County, est. 1811 (J-10)
Canal State Memorial in west central Franklin County (J-10)
State Park near Liberty, Indiana, Union County (J-10)
City Park at Richmond, Indiana, Wayne County (H-10)

The Delaware name for the scenic stream with its many rapids is Wapinepay or Wapi-nepaz meaning "white clear water." The headwaters of this swiftest river in Indiana are in Randolph County. The west and east forks merge at Brookville, Indiana, Franklin County. The fast moving river flows southeast to enter the state of Ohio, where it joins the Miami River, a tributary of the Ohio River near Cincinnati, Ohio.

Brookville Lake reservoir was established from the impounded waters of the Whitewater River East Fork, south of Whitewater Memorial State Park. Whitewater Canal State Memorial is located near the Whitewater River West Fork. Whitewater Gorge Park at Richmond, Indiana, features a hiking trail.

WILDCAT (WAILD-kat)
Creek in Howard, Carroll & Tippecanoe counties (E-F-5-6-7)
Township in northeast Tipton County, est. 1844 (F-7)

Miami Chief Godfroy stated that Wildcat Creek was named for Chief Richardville or "Wild Cat," whose Miami name was Pin-je-wah, Jean or John Baptiste Richardville, Pin-je-wah was the principal Miami Chief from 1814 to 1841, the year he died.

The Miami name for the stream was Pin-ji-wa-mo-tai meaning "belly of the wildcat" possibly in reference to the stream's flowing through Chief Richardville's vast reserve or the "the belly," center, or middle of his property. The French names for the stream included Rivare Pouextipecheaux, Ponceau Pichou, or Panse au Pichou.

Wildcat Creek is nearly 75 miles long heading in Howard County about a quarter mile north of West Liberty, Indiana. The stream flows northwest and west through Carroll County to the confluence at the Wabash River, about four miles north of Lafayette, Indiana, in Tippecanoe County. Tributaries include Little Wildcat Creek, Middle Fork Wildcat Creek, and South Fork Wildcat Creek. (see Russiaville)

WINAMAC (WIN-a-mack)
Town and County seat of Pulaski County, est. 1835 (D-6)
Fish & Wildlife Area, northeast Pulaski County (C-6)

Winamac, also spelled Winemac, Winnemack, Wynemac, Wynemack, Wen-e-megh, Wenamech, Wenamick, Winnimeg, and Quenemik means "catfish," derived from Algonquian wee-ned, "muddy," and mak, "fish." (Family Ictaluridae).

Several Potawatomi chiefs by the name of Winamac lived in northern Indiana during the first half of the nineteenth century, but most authorities are uncertain which chief the Pulaski County community is named.

According to local historian Richard Dodd, there are at least two Chief Winamacs that are historically documented; one hostile and one friendly to the United States during the War of 1812. However, it is believed a third friendly, virtually-unknown Chief Winamac at the time of the town's settlement is the source of the place name.

WINONA, WINONA LAKE (wa-NO-na)
Village in southeast Starke County, est. 1891 (C-8)
Town and lake in central Kosciusko County, est. 1898 (C-6)

Winona is derived from the Santee Dakota or Sioux proper name Wenonah, Wen-o-na, Wi-no-nah, or Wy-no-na meaning "first born," if a daughter. If the first born is a boy, the Siouan name was Chaskay.

The popular name Wenonah, the daughter of Nokomis ("grandmother"), came from Longfellow's epic poem. "Hiawatha." The name was also popularized by H.L. Gordon's 1881 poem, "Winona," and was adopted by Americans as a female personal name.

Winona, the village at the northeast edge of Bass Lake, was the first northern Indiana selection of the evangelical Winona Assembly for a spiritual retreat or Chautauqua. One hundred and sixty acres were purchased, but plans changed to move to Big Eagle Lake near Warsaw, Indiana, when the locals failed to come up with their share of railroad expense to build a rail spur from the main line at Bass Lake Station, north a few miles to the lake settlement.

Four years later in 1895, the Winona Assembly purchased the Kosciusko County location and changed the place name from Big Eagle Lake to Winona Lake. Tradition says Winona was the name of a favorite Potawatomi Indian princess. The long-standing symbol of Winona Lake has been an Indian princess head.

WOLF CREEK (WULF-kreek)
Twelve-mile stream in south central Marshall County (C-6)

Wolf Creek is a literal translation of the Potawatomi word, katam-wah-see-te-wah or ka-am-wah-see-te-wah meaning, "black wolf." McDonald reports in the **History of Marshall County,** "black wolves (Canis lupus) were numerous from one end of the creek to the other." Headwaters form near Argos, Indiana, and the Maxinkuckee morraine, east of Culver, Indiana, flowing northwest into Mill Pond, and eventually the Yellow River.

According to oral tradition, the Potawatomi waged war with the Fox and Miami to gain occupation. Potawatomi villages were then established along the stream which may have been named for their chief, Black Wolf.

WYALUSING CREEK (why-a-LUU-sing-kreek)
Stream in southwest Decatur & northwest Jennings counties (K-8-9)

Wyalusing is derived from the Delaware word, Michwigilusing or M'chiwihillusink meaning "old warrior's home" or "at the dwelling place of the hoary veteran." The place name is a transfer from a northeast Pennsylvania tributary of the Delaware-named Susquehanna River ("pure waters"), where a legendary Delaware warrior resided. Former Munsee, Delaware, and Iroquois settlements were located at the stream's mouth where the present-day community of Wyalusing, Bradford County, Pennsylvania, is located.

The Indiana stream is a tributary of Lekau-ahanne or "sand creek," the present-name. Scott, in his 1850 **Indiana Gazetteer** spelled the Delaware name as Laque-ka-ou-e-nik meaning "water running through sand." Sand Creek flows west to join with the White River East Fork in Bartholomew County.

WYANDOTTE (WINE-dot)
Caves in southeast Crawford County (N-6)
Village in southeast Crawford County, est. 1884 (N-6)
State Recreation Area in Harrison-Crawford State Forest (N-7)

The caves received their place name in 1852. Supposedly the caves obtained their present-day name from the former name of the nearby Blue River, once known as Windot Creek prior to 1800, named for the Indian tribe that resided along the stream.

The tribe of Wyandotte, Wyandot, or Windot is a name of Iroquoian linguistic stock. Perhaps Wendat comes the closest to the original word meaning "of one speech" or "people of the peninsula" or "islanders."

The Huron subtribe was originally from the islands in the St. Lawrence River and the peninsula between Lake Huron and

Georgian Bay, but fled west from Iroquois aggression in 1649. They were not members of the Iroquois Confederacy, but neither were the Hurons, Erie, and Cherokee, who also spoke a dialect of Iroquoian and felt the brunt of war. These once-eastern tribes now live in Kansas and Oklahoma.

Not only do Wyandotte Village, Wyandotte Woods State Recreation Area, and Wyandotte Caves bear a common name, but all of them are situated in close proximity to one another. (see Huron)

YANKEETOWN (YANG-ki-town)
Village in southeastern Warrick County, est. 1858 (O-3)

This Ohio River community was most likely named for the New England settlers or "yankees." The eastern settlers did not sympathize with the southern cause during the Antebellum Period and Civil War.

During the Colonial American period, the usage of the anglized form, "yankee," was more frequent in Virginia and the south. It is believed to be a derogratory nickname denoting cowardice, supposedly for the lack of armed support during an Indian uprising in Virginia, when New Englanders did not send support when called upon for assistance.

Yankee is a regional sobriquet or nickname of unknown origin, much like Hoosier. However, there is good evidence the name originated with a now-unknown Massachusetts Indian tribe who called the North European settlers, "yen-geese, yen-gis, yankis, or yankrvis," Indian names for "English."

YELLOW RIVER (YELL-low-river)
Stream of northwest Kosciusko, central Marshall & central Starke counties (C-5-6)

Yellow River is a near literal translation of the Potawatomi word for the stream, Wi-thou-gan, Way-thow-kah-nuk, or Wethananuk meaning "yellow waters" due to the high sand content of the streambed. The stream's headwaters begin in northwest Kosciusko County in an area known as Turkey Prairie.

The Yellow Branch or North Fork of the Yellow River flows from southeast St. Joseph County to join with the Yellow River at Bremen, Indiana. The Yellow Branch was known by the Potawatomi as po-co-nak meaning "beechy" for the high number of beech trees (Fagus grandifolia) growing along its banks.

The Yellow River continues its way through central Marshall

"Wi-thou-gan" or "yellow (river) waters"

County, south and west through the former reserve of Potawatomi Chief Menominee or "wild rice eater" near Twin Lakes Further on, Wythougan City Park in Knox, Indiana, is located along the south bank of the river on the community's northside. Beyond Knox, Indiana, the stream becomes dredged and channeled as it makes its way to the Kankakee River, near English Lake, Indiana, a total journey of 60 miles.

YORKTOWN (YORK-town)
Town in west central Delaware County, est. 1836 (G-9)

According to Sears, local historian and pioneer, Yorktown, Indiana, is supposedly named for a Delaware band from York, Pennsylvania. Evidence of a Indian village is found near the confluence of White River West Fork and Big Buck Creek at Yorktown; however, it is probably a Shawnee village.

HELPFUL LITERATURE

Anness, Milford E. **Song of Metamoris.** The Caxton Printers, Ltd., Caldwell, Idaho, 1964.

Anson, Bert. **The Miami Indians.** Norman, Oklahoma: University of Oklahoma Press, 1970.

Armstrong, M.A. **The Origin and Meaning of Place Names in Canada.** Toronto: The Macmillian Company of Canada, 1930.

Baker, Ronald and Carmony, Marvin. **Indiana Place Names.** Bloomington, Indiana: Indiana University Press, 1975.

Beauchamp, William M. **Aboriginal Places of New York.** Albany: New York State Education Department, 1907, 1971 rep.

Becker, Donald W. **Indian Place Names in New Jersey.** Cedar Grove, New Jersey: Phillips-Campbell Publishing Company, 1964.

Beckwith, Hiram Williams. **Indian Names of Water Courses in the State of Indiana.** Indiana Department of Geology and Natural History. Annual Report 12: 35-43, 1882.

Brinton, Daniel G., and Anthony, Rev. Albert S. **A Lenape-English Dictionary.** Philadelphia: The Historical Society of Pennsylvania, 1888.

Daggett, Rowann Keim. **Upper Wabash Valley Place Names: Wabash and Miami Counties.** Indiana University Ph.D. thesis: Bloomington, Indiana, 1978.

Donehoo, George P. **A History of the Indian Villages and Place Names in Pennsylvania.** Harrisburg, Pa.: The Telegraph Press, 1928, 1977 rep.

Dunlap, A. R., and Weslager, C. A. **Indian Place Names in Delaware.** Wilmington: Archaeological Society of Delaware, 1950.

Dunn, Jacob Piatt. **True Indian Stories.** North Manchester, Indiana; L. W. Shultz Publishing Company, 1908.

Dunn, Jacob Piatt. **True Indian Stories, with Glossary of Indiana Indian Names.** Indianapolis: Sentinel Printing Company, 1909.

Fitzpatrick, Lilian L. **Nebraska Place Names.** Lincoln: University of Nebraska Press, 1960.

Gard, Robert E., and Sorden, L. G. **The Romance of Wisconsin Place Names.** New York: October House, 1968.

Giorgiady, Nicholas P., Louis G. Romano, and Richard P. Klahn. **Indiana's First Settlers-The Indians.** Milwaukee: Franklin Publishers, Inc., 1968.

Guddle, Erwin G. **California Place Names.** Rev. ed. Berkeley: University of California Press, 1967.

Guernsey, E. Y. **Indiana; the Influence of the Indian Upon its History with Indian and French Names for Natural and Cultural Locations.** Indiana Conservation Department Publication n. (22), 1933 map.

Harder, Kelsie B. **The Illustrated Dictionary of Place Names:** United States and Canada. New York: Van Nostrand Reinhold, 1976.

Holmer, Nils Magus. **Indian Place Names in North America.** Cambridge: Harvard University Press, n.d.

Huden, John C. **Indian Place Names of New England.** New York: Museum of the American Indian, 1962.

Indiana Historical Society. **Indians and a Changing Frontier: The Art of George Winter.** Indiana Historical Society: Indianapolis, Ind., 1993.

Kenny, Hamill. **West Virgina Place Names.** Piedmont, W. Va.: The Place Name Press, 1945.

Kinietz, W. Vernon. **The Indians of the Western Great Lakes, 1615-1760.** Ann Arbor: University of Michigan Press, 1963.

Lockridge, Ross F. **Indian Names of Indiana Streams.** Indiana Teacher, April 1945 p. 215-16.

McArthur, Lewis A. **Oregon Geographic Names.** 4th ed. rev. Portland: Oregon Historical Society, 1974.

"Names of Indian Streams." Indiana History Bulletin, 9: 543-45, August 1932.

Phillips, James W. **Alaska-Yukon Place Names.** Seattle: University of Washington Press, 1973.

Pizer, Vernon. **Ink, Arkansas, and all that: How American Places Got their Names.** New York: Putnam, 1976.

Place Name Index. Indianapolis: Indiana Historical Society Library.

Read, William A. **Florida Place Names of Indian Origin and Seminole Personal Names.** Baton Rouge: Louisiana State University Press, 1934.

Read, William A. **Indian Place Names in Alabama.** Rev. ed. Tuscaloosa: University of Alabama Press, 1937, rep. 1984.

Rydjord, John. **Indian Place Names.** Norman: University of Oklahoma Press, 1968, rep. 1972.

Shirk, George H. **Oklahoma Place Names.** 2nd edition revised. Norman: University of Oklahoma Press, 1974.

Shultz, L. W., and Lamb, E. Wendall. **Indian Lore.** North Manchester, Indiana: L.W. Shultz Publishing Company, 1968.

Shultz, L. W., and Lamb, E. Wendall. **More Indian Lore.** North Manchester, Indiana: L. W. Schultz Publishing Company, 1968.

Sneve, Virginia Driving Hawk. **South Dakota Geographic Names.** Sioux Falls, S. D.: Brevet Press, 1973.

Stewart, George R. **American Place Names.** New York: Oxford University Press, 1970.

Tooker, William W. **The Indian Place Names on Long Island.** reprint. Port Washington, New York: Ira J. Freidman, 1962.

Upham, Warren. **Minnesota Georgraphical Names.** St. Paul: Minnesota Historical Society, 1969.

Urbanek, Mae. **Wyoming Place Names.** Boulder, Colorado: Johnson Publishing Company, 1974.

Various Indiana County History Books.

Voggelin, Carl F. **Shawnee Stems.** Indianapolis: Indiana Historical Society, n.d.

Vogel, Virgil J. **Indian Names in Michigan.** Ann Arbor: University of Michigan Press, 1968.

Vogel, Virgil J. **Indian Names in Iowa.** Iowa City: University of Iowa Press, 1983.

Vogel, Virgil J. **Indian Place Names in Illinois.** Springfield, Illinois State Historical Society, 1963.

Weslager, C. A. **The Delaware Indians, A History.** New Brunswick, New Jersey: Rutgers University Press, 1972.

Winger, Otto. **Last of the Miamis.** North Manchester, Indiana: L. W. Schultz Publishing Company, 1968.

Winger, Otto. **The Potawatomi Indians.** North Manchester, Indiana: L. W. Schultz Publishing Company, 1968.

**SUBJECT INDEX: Indian Names in Indiana;
Counties, Townships, Communities, Schools,
Parks, Lakes & Streams**

INDIANA COUNTIES/INDIAN NAMES

Delaware	Tippecanoe
Elkhart	Vermillion
Miami	Wabash
Ohio	Wells

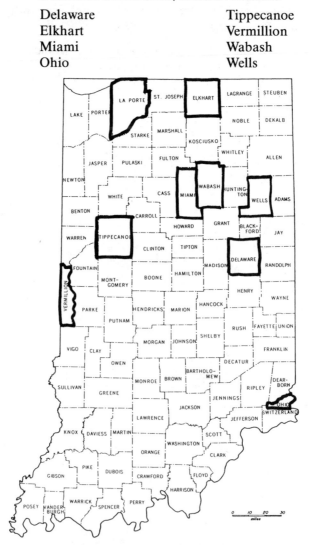

**Map 3: Indiana Counties with
Indian and Indian-Related Names**

"Appeal to the Great Spirit," Culver Academy Grounds, Culver, Indiana

INDIANA TOWNSHIPS/INDIAN NAMES

Anderson — Madison County
Aubbeenaubee — Fulton County
Baugo — Elkhart County
Beanblossom — Monroe County
Calumet — Lake County
Cedar Creek — Allen County
Clifty Creek — Bartholomew County
Deer Creek — Miami, Cass, & Carroll counties
Delaware — Delaware, Hamilton, & Ripley counties
Driftwood — Jackson County
Eel River, north — Allen & Cass counties
Eel River, south — Hendricks County
Elkhart — Noble & Elkhart counties
Erie — Miami County

INDIAN TOWNSHIPS/INDIAN NAMES (continued)

Fall Creek — Henry, Madison & Hamilton counties
Flat Rock — Bartholomew County
Indian Creek — Lawrence, Monroe & Pulaski counties
Iroquois — Newton County
Kankakee — LaPorte & Jasper counties
Lagro — Wabash County
Maumee — Allen County
Miami — Miami & Cass counties
Michigan City, Michigantown — LaPorte & Clinton counties
Monon — White County
Ohio — Crawford, Bartholomew, Spencer, & Warrick counties
Oregon — Clark & Starke counties
Otsego — Steuben County
Patoka — Crawford, Dubois, Gibson, & Pike counties
Parish Grove — Benton County
Paw Paw — Wabash County
Peru — Miami County
Raccoon — Parke County
Salamonie — Huntington County
Saluda — Jefferson County
Shawnee — Fountain County
Sugar Creek — Boone, Clinton, Montgomery, & Parke counties
Tippecanoe — Kosciusko, Marshall, Pulaski & Tippecanoe counties
Trail Creek — LaPorte County
Vermillion — Vermillion County
Wabash — Jay, Fountain, Adams, Tippecanoe, Parke, & Gibson counties
Wea — Tippecanoe County
White River — Hamilton, Johnson, & Gibson counties
Whitewater — Franklin County
Wildcat — Tipton County

INDIANA COMMUNITIES/INDIAN NAMES

Amboy — Miami County
Anderson — Madison County
Anoka — Cass County
Beanblossom — Brown County
Black Hawk — Vigo County
Burnettsville — White County
Cayuga — Vermillion County
Chili — Miami County

INDIANA COMMUNITIES/INDIAN NAMES (continued)

Churubusco — Whitley County
Coesse — Whitley County
Cornstalk — Howard County
Cuba — Allen & Owen counties
Cuzco — Dubois County
Deer Creek — Carroll County
Delaware — Ripley County
Door Village — LaPorte County
East Chicago, New Chicago — Lake County
Elkhart — Elkhart County
Erie — Miami & Lawrence counties
Georgetown — Cass County
Greentown — Howard County
Huron — Lawrence County
Indian Heights — Howard County
Indian Springs — Martin County
Indian Village — Noble & St. Joseph counties
Indianapolis — Marion County
Jalapa — Grant County
Kappa — Howard County
Kewanna — Fulton County
Klondike — Tippecanoe & Parke counties
Klondyke — Vermillion County
Kokomo — Howard County
LaCrosse — LaPorte County
LaFontaine — Wabash County
Lagro — Wabash County
Logansport — Cass County
Majenica — Huntington County
Manhattan — Putnam County
Maumee — Jackson County
Maxinkuckee — Marshall County
Metamora — Franklin County
Metea — Cass County
Mexico — Miami County
Miami — Miami County
Michiana Shores — LaPorte County
Michigan City — LaPorte County
Michigantown — Clinton County
Mishawaka — St. Jospeh County

INDIANA COMMUNTIES/INDIAN NAMES (continued)

INDIANA COMMUNITIES/INDIAN NAMES (continued)

Wakarusa — Elkhart County
Wanatah, South Wanatah — LaPorte County
Wawasee — Kosciusko County
Wawaka — Noble County
Wawpecong — Miami County
Wea-ton, Wea-town — Tippecanoe County
White Cloud — Harrison County
Whitewater — Wayne County
Winamac — Pulaski County
Winona — Starke County
Winona Lake — Kosciusko County
Wyandotte — Crawford County
Yankeetown — Warrick County
Yorktown — Delaware County

INDIANA SCHOOLS/INDIAN NAMES

Anderson Elementary, High & Vocational — Anderson, Indiana
Calumet High — Gary, Indiana
Cayuga Elementary — Cayuga, Indiana
Churubusco Elementary & High — Churubusco, Indiana
Clifty Creek Elementary — Columbus, Indiana
Coesse Elementary — Columbia City, Indiana
Delaware Elementary — Evansville, Indiana
Delaware Youth Center — Indianapolis, Indiana
East Chicago Central High — East Chicago, Indiana
Elkhart Central & Memorial High, Area Career Center — Elkhart, Indiana
Fall Creek Elementary — Fishers, Indiana
Indian Creek Elementary, Intermediate, High — Trafalgar, Indiana
Indian Heights — Kokomo, Indiana
Indian Meadows Elementary — Ft. Wayne, Indiana
Indian Trail Elementary — LaPorte, Indiana
Indian Village Elementary — Fort Wayne, Indiana
Kankakee Valley Middle & High — Wheatfield, Indiana
Kekionga Middle — Fort Wayne, Indiana
Killbuck Elementary — Anderson, Indiana
Klondike Elementary — West Lafayette, Indiana
Kokomo High (Downtown & South), Area Career Center — Kokomo, Indiana
LaCrosse Elementary & High — LaCrosse, Indiana
LaFontaine Elementary — LaFontaine, Indiana
Logansport High, Area Joint Special Education — Logansport, Indiana

INDIANA SCHOOLS/INDIAN NAMES (continued)

INDIANA PARKLANDS/INDIAN NAMES

Ferrettie - Baugo Creek County Park — St. Joseph County
Kankakee Fish & Wildlife Area — Starke & LaPorte counties
Kilsoquah State Recreation Area - Huntington Lake Reservoir — Huntington County
Little Turtle State Recreation Area - Huntington Lake Reservoir — Huntington County
Maconaquah City Park — Peru, Indiana, Miami County
Menominee Public Fishing Area — Fulton County
Menominee Wetlands Conservation Area — Marshall County
Metea County Park — Allen County
Minnehaha Fish & Wildlife Area — Sullivan County
Mixsawbah State Fish Hatchery — LaPorte County
Pokagon State Park — Steuben County
Potawatomi Wildlife Park — Marshall County
Potawatomi Zoo — South Bend, Indiana, St. Joseph County
Raccoon State Recreation Area — Parke County
Salamonie Reservoir & State Forest — Wabash & Huntington counties
Shakamak State Park — Greene County
Tippecanoe River State Park — Pulaski County
Ouabache State Park — Wells County
Whitewater Canal State Memorial — Franklin County
Whitewater State Park — Union County
Winamac Fish & Wildlife Area — Pulaski County
Wyandotte Caves — Crawford County
Wyandotte Woods State Recreation Area — Harrison & Crawford counties
Wythougan City Park — Knox, Indiana, Starke County

INDIAN LAKES/INDIAN NAMES

Beanblossom Lake or Lake Lemon — Monroe & Brown counties
Indian Lake — DeKalb County
Lake Cicott — Cass County
Lake Lenape — Greene County
Lake Manitou — Fulton County
Lake Maxinkuckee — Marshal County
Lake Michigan — LaPorte, Porter, & Lake counties
Lake Tippecanoe — Kosciusko County
Lake Wawasee — Kosciusko County
Mississinewa Reservoir/Lake — Grant, Wabash, & Miami counties
Muncie Lake — Noble County
Muskelonge Lake — Kosciusko County
Oswego Lake — Kosciusko County
Papakeechie Lake — Kosciusko County
Potoka Reservoir/Lake — Orange & Dubois counties
Pottawatomie Lake — LaPorte County

INDIANA LAKES/INDIAN NAMES (continued)

Salamonie Reservoir/Lake — Huntington & Wabash counties
Shakamak Lake — Greene County
Shipshewana Lake — Lagrange County
Waubee Lake — Kosciusko County
Winona Lake — Kosciusko County

INDIANA STREAMS/INDIAN NAMES

Baugo Creek — Elkhart & St. Joseph counties
Beanblossom Creek — Brown & Monroe counties
Ben Davis Fork — Rush County
Burnetts Creek — Cass, White, & Tippecanoe counties
Calumet, Grand & Little — LaPorte, Porter, & Lake counties
Cedar Creek — Dekalb & Allen counties
Charley Creek — Wabash County
Chippewanuck Creek — Kosciusko & Fulton counties
Clifty Creek — Rush, Decatur, & Bartholomew counties
Cornstalk Creek — Howard & Montgomery counties
Deer Creek — Miami, Howard, Cass, & Carroll counties
Driftwood River — Johnson & Bartholomew counties
Eel River, north — Allen, Whitley, Wabash, & Miami counties
Eel River, south — Putnam, Clay, Owen, & Greene counties
Elkhart River — Noble, Lagrange, & Elkhart counties
Fall Creek — Henry, Madison, Hamilton, & Marion counties
Flat Rock River — Henry, Rush, Decatur, Shelby, & Bartholomew counties
Flowers Creek — Miami County
Hurricane Creek (6) Rush & Decatur; Dubois & Perry; Spencer; Wells; Whitley, &
    Kosciusko; Johnson counties
Indian Creek (16) sixteen scattered streams throughout state (see page 22)
Indian-Kentuck Creek — Jefferson County
Iroquois River — Jasper & Newton counties
Kankakee River — St. Joseph, LaPorte, Starke, Porter, Jasper, Lake, &
    Newton counties
Kickapoo Creek — Warren County
Killbuck Creek — Delaware & Madison counties
Kokomo Creek — Howard County
Lagro Creek-Wabash County
Majenica Creek — Huntington County
Maumee River — Allen County
Metocinah or Josina Creek — Grant & Miami counties
Mississinewa River — Delaware, Grant, Wabash, & Miami counties

INDIANA STREAMS/INDIAN NAMES (continued)

Muncie Creek — Delaware County

Muscatatuck River — Jefferson, Jennings, Scott, Washington, & Jackson counties

Ohio River — Dearborn, Ohio, Switzerland, Jefferson, Clark, Floyd, Harrison, Crawford, Perry, Spencer, Warrick, & Vanderburgh counties

Opossum Creek & Opossum Run — Brown & Warren counties

Patoka River — Orange, Dubois, Pike, & Gibson counties

Paw Paw Creek — Wabash, Miami & Cass counties

Pigeon River — Steuben & Lagrange counties

Pipe Creek — Delaware, Madison & Hamilton; Grant, Miami & Cass counties; Ripley & Franklin counties

Raccoon Creek, Big & Little-Boone, Montgomery, Owen, Parke, Putnam counties; Ripley County

Salamonie River — Jay, Blackford, Wells, Huntington, & Wabash counties

Saluda Creek — Jefferson County

Shankitunk/Shankatank Creek — Henry & Rush counties

Shawnee Creek, Big & Little — Tippecanoe & Fountain; Rush & Fayette counties

Shipshewana Creek — Lagrange County

Squirrel Creek — Miami & Wabash counties

Sugar Creek — Clinton, Boone, Montgomery, & Parke counties

Tippecanoe River — Kosciusko, Marshall, Fulton, Pulaski, White, Carroll, & Tippecanoe counties

Trail Creek — LaPorte County

Vermillion River, Big & Little — Vermillion County

Wabash River — Adams, Wells, Huntington, Wabash, Miami, Cass, Carroll, Tippecanoe, Warren, Fountain, Vermillion, Parke, Vigo, Sullivan, Knox, Gibson, & Posey counties

Little Wabash or Little River — Allen & Huntington counties

Wea Creek, Big & Little — Tippecanoe County

Weasel/Weasaw Creek — Miami County

White River — Pike, Gibson, & Knox counties

White River East Fork — Bartholomew, Jackson, Washington, Lawrence, Martin, Dubois, Pike, & Daviess

White River West Fork — Randolph, Delaware, Madison, Hamilton, Marion, Johnson, Morgan, Monroe, Owen, Greene, Daviess, & Knox counties

Whitewater, East & West Forks-Randolph, Wayne, Fayette, Union, Franklin, & Dearborn counties

Wildcat Creek — Howard, Carroll, & Tippecanoe counties

Wolf Creek — Marshall County

Wyalusing Creek — Decatur & Jennings counties

Yellow River — Kosciusko, Marshall, & Starke counties

INDIANA COUNTIES WITH INDIAN INFLUENCE

Allen
Carroll
Cass
Crawford
Daviess
Delaware
Elkhart
Fountain
Fulton
Grant
Hamilton
Howard
Huntington
Jefferson

Kosciusko
Lagrange
LaPorte
Madison
Marshall
Miami
Noble
Pulaski
St. Joseph
Tippecanoe
Wabash
White
Whitley

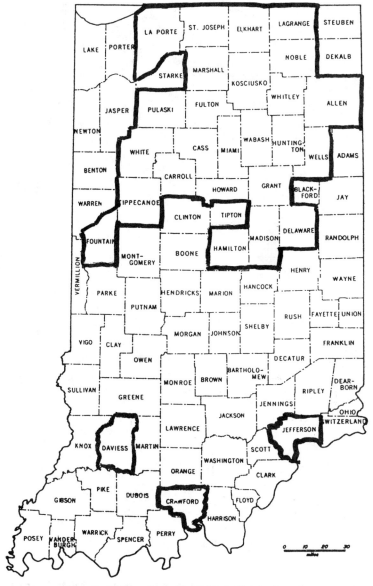

Map 4: Indiana Counties With Indian Influence

Map 5: Indiana's Major Streams with Indian or Indian-Related Names

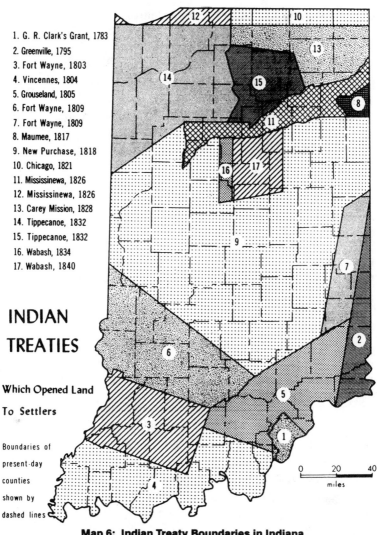

1. G. R. Clark's Grant, 1783
2. Greenville, 1795
3. Fort Wayne, 1803
4. Vincennes, 1804
5. Grouseland, 1805
6. Fort Wayne, 1809
7. Fort Wayne, 1809
8. Maumee, 1817
9. New Purchase, 1818
10. Chicago, 1821
11. Mississinewa, 1826
12. Mississinewa, 1826
13. Carey Mission, 1828
14. Tippecanoe, 1832
15. Tippecanoe, 1832
16. Wabash, 1834
17. Wabash, 1840

INDIAN

TREATIES

Which Opened Land

To Settlers

Boundaries of
present-day
counties
shown by
dashed lines

0   20   40
miles

Map 6: Indian Treaty Boundaries in Indiana
Map by Robert C. Kingsbury

**COUNTY INDEX: Indian Names In Indiana;
Counties, Townships, Communities, Parks, Lakes & Streams**

CLAY COUNTY

Eel River, south

CLINTON COUNTY

Michigantown, Indiana
Michigantown Township
Sugar Creek
Sugar Creek Township

CRAWFORD COUNTY

Ohio River
Ohio Township
Patoka Township
Wyandotte, Indiana
Wyandotte Caves
Wyandotte Woods State Rec. Area

DAVIESS COUNTY

Waco, Indiana
White River
White River East Fork
White River West Fork

DEARBORN COUNTY

Ohio River
White Eye Trail
Whitewater River

DECATUR COUNTY

Clifty Creek
Flat Rock River
Little Hurricane Creek
Sandusky, Indiana
Wyalusing Creek

DEKALB COUNTY

Cedar Creek
Indian Lake

DELAWARE COUNTY

Delaware County
Delaware Township
Killbuck Creek
Missisinewa River
Muncie, Indiana
Muncie Creek
Pipe Creek
White River West Fork
Yorktown, Indiana

DUBOIS COUNTY

Cuzco, Indiana
Hurricane Creek
Indian Creek
Patoka River
Patoka Lake/Reservoir
Patoka Township
White River East Fork

ELKHART COUNTY

Baugo Creek
Baugo Township
Elkhart County
Elkhart, Indiana
Elkhart River
Elkhart Township
Nappanee, Indiana
Wakarusa, Indiana

FAYETTE COUNTY

Shawnee Creek
Whitewater River West Fork

FLOYD COUNTY

Indian Creek
Ohio River